Scarecrow Studies in Young Adult Literature
Series Editor: Patty Campbell

Scarecrow Studies in Young Adult Literature is intended to continue the body of critical writing established in Twayne's Young Adult Authors Series and to expand it beyond single-author studies to explorations of genres, multicultural writing, and controversial issues in young adult (YA) reading. Many of the contributing authors of the series are among the leading scholars and critics of adolescent literature, and some are YA novelists themselves.

The series is shaped by its editor, Patty Campbell, who is a renowned authority in the field, with a thirty-year background as critic, lecturer, librarian, and teacher of YA literature. Patty Campbell was the 2001 winner of the ALAN Award, given by the Assembly on Adolescent Literature of the National Council of Teachers of English for distinguished contribution to YA literature. In 1989 she was the winner of the American Library Association's Grolier Award for distinguished service to young adults and reading.

1. *What's So Scary about R. L. Stine?* by Patrick Jones, 1998.
2. *Ann Rinaldi: Historian and Storyteller*, by Jeanne M. McGlinn, 2000.
3. *Norma Fox Mazer: A Writer's World*, by Arthea J. S. Reed, 2000.
4. *Exploding the Myths: The Truth about Teens and Reading*, by Marc Aronson, 2001.
5. *The Agony and the Eggplant: Daniel Pinkwater's Heroic Struggles in the Name of YA Literature*, by Walter Hogan, 2001.
6. *Caroline Cooney: Faith and Fiction*, by Pamela Sissi Carroll, 2001.
7. *Declarations of Independence: Empowered Girls in Young Adult Literature, 1990–2001*, by Joanne Brown and Nancy St. Clair, 2002.
8. *Lost Masterworks of Young Adult Literature*, by Connie S. Zitlow, 2002.
9. *Beyond the Pale: New Essays for a New Era*, by Marc Aronson, 2003.
10. *Orson Scott Card: Writer of the Terrible Choice*, by Edith S. Tyson, 2003.
11. *Jacqueline Woodson: "The Real Thing,"* by Lois Thomas Stover, 2003.
12. *Virginia Euwer Wolff: Capturing the Music of Young Voices*, by Suzanne Elizabeth Reid, 2003.

Sisters, Schoolgirls, and Sleuths

Girls' Series Books in America

Carolyn Carpan

Scarecrow Studies in Young Adult Literature, No. 30

The Scarecrow Press, Inc.
Lanham, Maryland • Toronto • Plymouth, UK
2009

SCARECROW PRESS, INC.

Published in the United States of America by Scarecrow Press, Inc.
A wholly owned subsidary of The Rowman & Littlefield Publishing Group, Inc.
4501 Forbes Boulevard, Suite 200, Lanham, Maryland 20706
www.scarecrowpress.com

Estover Road
Plymouth PL6 7PY
United Kingdom

British Library Cataloguing in Publication Information Available

Library of Congress Cataloging-in-Publication Data

Carpan, Carolyn.
  Sisters, schoolgirls, and sleuths : girls' series books in America / Carolyn
Carpan.
      p. cm. — (Scarecrow studies in young adult literature ; no. 30)
    Includes bibliographical references and index.
    ISBN-13: 978-0-8108-5756-8 (alk. paper)
    ISBN-10: 0-8108-5756-1 (alk. paper)
    ISBN-13: 978-0-8108-6395-8 (ebook)
    ISBN-10: 0-8108-6395-2 (ebook)
  1. Children's stories, American–History and criticism. 2. Young adult fiction,
American–History and criticism. 3. Girls in literature. 4. Teenage girls in fiction.
5. Children's literature in series–History and criticism. 6. Girls–Books and
reading–United States–History. I. Title.
  PS374.G55C37 2009
  813'.50992827–dc22   2008036693

♾™ The paper used in this publication meets the minimum requirements of
American National Standard for Information Sciences—Permanence of
Paper for Printed Library Materials, ANSI/NISO Z39.48–1992.
Manufactured in the United States of America.

For all my friends who have enjoyed reading girls' series books

Contents

Acknowledgments

I want to thank all my colleagues at Rollins College and the Olin Library for their support for this book. I especially want to acknowledge Shawne Keevan, circulation/interlibrary loan specialist, for her work in tracking down books and articles for me. Her persistence found me several older girls' series books I didn't ever expect to read. Thank you to the rest of the circulation staff in the Olin Library for their assistance with these interlibrary loans. I also want to thank Patricia Grall, circulation/periodicals specialist, for loaning me her precious Janet Lambert books. Thanks also to Dr. Yvonne Jones, reference librarian and assistant professor, who loaned me her Nancy Drew books.

Thank you to Rollins College for granting me Jack B. Critchfield research funds. With this funding, I was able to travel to research collections and purchase books needed to complete my research.

I'd like to thank Ann Hudak, assistant curator in the Marylandia and Rare Books Department for the University of Maryland Libraries, for her assistance and hospitality when I visited the Pagnani Collection of girls' series books at the Hornbake Library.

I owe a big thank you to my series editor, Patty Campbell, who knew it was time for a genre study and social history of girls' series books. Her enthusiasm for my book never failed, and it sometimes kept me going. It has been a pleasure working with Patty.

Finally, thanks to all of my friends who have enjoyed reading girls' series books and for talking to me about them over the years. You know who you are.

Introduction

For more than a century and a half, girls across the United States have read series books written just for them. When I mention my interest in girls' series, a woman in the group always exclaims with a smile, "Oh, I loved Nancy Drew!" or "I remember Sweet Valley High!" Readers remember their favorite girls' series books with great affection. Common themes found in girls' series include friendship, family, adventure, mystery, and romance.

Girls' series books allow readers to enter a world where the action centers on the girls. Readers come to think of the main characters in their favorite girls' series as their friends, and the series remain popular because readers don't want to miss out on their friends' fun. The characters in girls' series books often have more freedom than their readers, allowing readers to vicariously experience exciting adventures, whether the protagonist and her friends are going to the high school prom or to the local haunted house to solve a mystery.

Many series feature wealthy girls who have every material thing a girl could ever want. If the protagonist is from a middle or lower class family, she often befriends a rich girl who shares her luxurious lifestyle and social status with her friends. The poor protagonist proves she is worthy by obeying and protecting the system, rather than challenging it. Scholar Peter Stoneley argues,

> Series fiction is both outside and inside wealth, offering a vicarious luxury to the reader while establishing the boundaries of the leisure class. . . . The fiction . . . lays bare its founding contradiction: An enormous hunger for wealth and status is expressed, while climbers and interlopers are exposed and punished.[1]

Moreover, given these social divisions, Stoneley suggests, "the narratives incite a strong motivation in the girl-reader: She had better make sure that she belongs."[2] Reading girls' series books featuring wealthy and popular girls allow readers to feel like they belong, while ensuring that girls understand and obey the rules of the system. Although this is certainly a condemnation of girls' series, and indeed why some girls choose not to read them, it's important to acknowledge that girls' series books are also fun to read. Many readers realize contemporary girls' series fiction is fantasy, not reality, and they enjoy the escape from their own lives that reading series offers them.

What exactly are series books? Series books are defined as "a sequence of separate narratives, mostly about the same characters and usually written by one author" or ghostwriters under a pseudonym.[3] Progressive series develop a story in sequential installments, while books in successive series can be read in any order, since each plot is separate and characters don't age or change. A few key series are published under a series title and logo, with different characters appearing in each book. For the purposes of this study, the number of books in a series can be anywhere from three to 300. Usually a series written by a single author has fewer titles, while series written by many authors or ghostwriters feature many titles. Series books generally follow a formula, and so each story in a series and genre resembles each other. But this is precisely *why* readers read series books. Teens and preteens know what they will get when they read series books, whether they are reading the religious Elsie Dinsmore series, Nancy Drew mysteries, or such high school series as Sweet Valley High or Gossip Girl. Scholar Catherine Sheldrick Ross argues,

> Reading a series book is said to be like eating a MacDonald's hamburger—a standardized commodity lacking in surprise. But for the child

reader, as for the fast food purchaser, there is an advantage in knowing what you are going to get.[4]

Librarians, teachers, and parents have usually scorned series books, citing the predictable formula, lack of character development, and simple plots. But Ross contends, "For many readers, series books may provide the clearest initiation into the rules of reading because as fictions they are highly patterned."[5] By reading the formula over and over again, readers learn basic information about how book plots are structured. In fact, "committed readers so often say that series books introduced them to the joy of reading."[6] Reading stories they enjoy can make children and teens lifelong readers.

Another criticism of series books focuses on the unrealistic lives led by protagonists and their friends. For instance, Elsie Dinsmore inherits a large amount of money upon her marriage, enabling her to travel and support her large extended family during the Civil War. Nosy Nancy Drew chases thieves and con artists worldwide, and her adventures are amply funded by her loving father. Gossip Girls Blair and Serena party with their friends in New York City's hottest clubs, sporting the latest fashions and gadgets bought for them by their wealthy parents. While girls enjoy reading about the exciting adventures of their fictional friends, they are drawn to the stories because they know they are unrealistic. Contemporary series books, for most readers, are fantastic adventures featuring affluent girls whose lives are very different from their own. The fact that the stories are fantasy appeals to readers. For more than a century and a half, many preteen and teen girls have chosen to read series books when they are able to choose their own recreational reading material. Since the mid-nineteenth century, girls' series books have introduced readers to wealthy sisters, schoolgirls, and sleuths who have exciting adventures time and again.

First published in 1867, Martha Finley's Elsie Dinsmore series enthralled readers who followed Elsie's life from childhood to widowhood, as she struggled to tame her emotional nature and become a lady worthy of her wealth and position in society. In the early twentieth century, during the heyday of American women's colleges, girls' high school and college stories like Betty Wales, Grace Harlowe, The Girls of Central High, and Jane Allen were popular with teen readers.

From 1910 and 1920, there was a huge growth in the number of girls' series books, and many of these new stories were modeled after boys' adventure stories. The Stratemeyer Syndicate, a fiction factory that hired ghostwriters to write from founder Edward Stratemeyer's outlines, published many series books for boys and girls. The new adventure girls, like The Automobile Girls, The Motor Girls, and The Girl Aviators, rode around in motorcars and airplanes, traveling farther from home and gaining a measure of independence. The beloved Outdoor Girls used their feet, finding adventures while they walked the countryside.

In the 1910s, an important series that blended the genres of many girls' series together featured Ruth Fielding as an orphan, a school and college girl, a brave adventurer, a career-minded businesswoman, and a loving wife and mother. The Ruth Fielding series also introduced the mystery genre to girls' series books, which readers loved so much that the plucky amateur sleuth Nancy Drew became the most beloved girls' series heroine when she debuted in 1930. Series like Cherry Ames, Beverly Gray, and Vicki Barr introduced girls to careers during World War II, but even career girls have time to play detective. Young sleuth Trixie Belden was a refreshing change from the career girls and the older, bolder Nancy Drew.

During the postwar 1940s and 1950s, there was a rise in romance fiction for teen girls, following the publication of Maureen Daly's romantic *Seventeenth Summer*. Romantic family series like Janet Lambert's Parrish Family stories, along with Rosamund Du Jardin's series about the lives and loves of sisters Tobey and Midge Heydon and twins Pam and Penny Howard, were popular with teen girls. Mysteries remained popular, and career girls solved more mysteries and worked less. Nancy Drew underwent a makeover to eliminate racial stereotypes, shorten the books, and transform Nancy into a shadow of her former self.

The new Nancy Drew pushed other beloved girl detectives, like Judy Bolton and Cherry Ames, out of the market by the late 1960s. The Stratemeyer Syndicate dominated the girls' series book market throughout the 1960s and 1970s. Ironically, the diluted Nancy Drew introduced in the late 1950s became a second wave feminist icon in the 1970s, boosted by a short-lived television show based on the books.

As a reaction to the second wave of feminism, teen romance fiction was revived in the early 1980s, and romance series dominated the decade. Such single-title series as Wildfire and continuing soap-opera romances as Sweet Valley High were popular. A Sweet Valley High Super Edition book, *Perfect Summer*, was the first teen novel to rank on the *New York Times* bestseller list. In response to the popularity of her series, Sweet Valley High creator Francine Pascal launched a variety of spin-off series for preteen and teen readers.

During the 1990s, when the horror genre became popular in films and adult fiction, horror series fiction caught the attention of both teen girls and boys. Girls gobbled up gory thrillers like R. L. Stine's Fear Street and Christopher Pike's Chain Letter. Soap-opera romances, like Sweet Valley High and the spin-off series SVH Senior Year, continued to capture the attention of teen and tween girls who still wanted to read romances. Series about girls with unusual powers, like Francine Pascal's Fearless, were popular in the late 1990s as the third wave of feminism helped make girl power a part of American popular culture. By the early twenty-first century, however, such series about spoiled rich teens as Gossip Girl, The A-List, Private, and The Clique were so popular they were making the *New York Times* bestseller list.

Girls' series books have been the subject of book-length scrutiny for several decades. Acclaimed author Bobbie Ann Mason wrote about American girls' series books, highlighting the genre in her witty memoir *The Girl Sleuth* in 1975. In the mid-1980s, writer Carol Billman published *The Secret of the Stratemeyer Syndicate*, detailing Edward Stratemeyer's children's fiction factory. Her fascinating book provides an overview of the Stratemeyer Syndicate business and includes lengthy studies of the Nancy Drew and Ruth Fielding series.

During the 1990s, following the first scholarly Nancy Drew Conference in Iowa in 1993, girls' series fiction became regarded as a worthy research topic by academics and writers. Scholar Deidre Johnson published her excellent study, *Edward Stratemeyer and the Stratemeyer Syndicate*, which includes chapters about girls' and mystery series. Later in the decade, Sherrie A. Inness edited a wonderful collection of scholarly articles about girls' series books in *Nancy Drew and Company*, while bestselling authors Carole Kismaric and Marvin Heiferman published a lighter look at the Stratemeyer Syndicate's popular series in *The Mysterious Case of Nancy Drew and The Hardy Boys*. To mark the seventy-fifth anniversary of the Nancy Drew series in 2005, writer Melanie Rehak published a fascinating biography of Stratemeyer Syndicate head Harriet Adams and ghostwriter Mildred Wirt in *Girl Sleuth: Nancy Drew and the Women Who Created Her*. In the late twentieth and early twenty-first centuries, academics interested in the study of literature and culture also published numerous articles focusing on girls' series books.

While the Nancy Drew mystery series has commanded the lion's share of attention, scholars, librarians, and book collectors have also published books about other prominent girls' series. Scholar Linda Christian-Smith studied the content of 1950s and 1980s teen romance series in *Becoming a Woman through Romance*. A girls' series fan group, the Society of Phantom Friends, published *The Girls' Series Companion*, an annotated guide to girls' series. Librarian Silk Makowski published *Serious about Series*, evaluating and annotating many series for teen girls published in the 1980s and 1990s. Girls' series book collector John Axe also published two books in the early twenty-first century focusing on book collecting in *The Secret of Collecting Girls' Series Books* and *All about Collecting Girls' Series Books*. Although Axe's writing is sometimes weak, his knowledge about the various editions and printings, along with the color pictures of cover art, make these books invaluable for anyone who wants to learn about girls' series books published in the first half of the twentieth century. No one, however, has studied girls' series books as a genre from its beginnings. It is time for a chronological social history of American girls' series books examining how young women are portrayed and how the series are both a product and vehicle of popular culture.

Notes

1. Peter Stoneley, *Consumerism and American Girls' Literature*, *1860–1940* (Cambridge, U.K.: Cambridge University Press, 2003), 95.

2. Stoneley, *Consumerism and American Girls' Literature*, 97.

3. Victor Watson, "Series Books," *The Oxford Encyclopedia of Children's Literature*, Vol. 1, ed. Jack Zipes (New York: Oxford University Press, 2006), 437.

4. Catherine Sheldrick Ross, "If They Read Nancy Drew, So What?: Series Book Readers Talk Back," *Library and Information Science Research*, 17 (1995): 222.

5. Ross, "If They Read Nancy Drew, So What?" 230.

6. Ross, "If They Read Nancy Drew, So What?" 202.

1

✆

Victorian and Vassar Girls: Nineteenth-Century Origins of Girls' Series Fiction

The origins of girls' series fiction can be found in nineteenth-century children's literature, which drew on such literary movements as romanticism and sentimentalism. As a response to eighteenth-century rationalism, romanticism and sentimentalism focused on emotion rather than intellect and reason. Sentimentalism was associated with true virtue, and an "adherence to strict morality and honor, combined with copious feeling and a sympathetic heart, were . . . the marks of the man or woman" or child of sentiment.[1] By the end of the nineteenth century, the child in children's fiction, once "rational, sober, and imperfect at the beginning of the nineteenth century, had become innocent, charming, and perfect: The rational had become the romantic child."[2]

Children's series fiction, beginning in the 1830s, quickly became a vehicle for promoting an idealized, romantic Victorian child. The emphasis in Martha Finley's Elsie Dinsmore series is on sentiment and the power of the young, innocent female heroine to redeem everyone around her, which put this most popular girls' series of the nineteenth century firmly in the romantic and sentimental traditions when the series began in 1867. Scholar Pam Hardman argues, however, that the Elsie Dinsmore series shifts quickly away from romanticism and sentimentalism to a "pragmatic, worldly Victorianism."[3] The Elsie Dinsmore series, which continued for thirty-eight years, changed from sentimental, romantic stories to practical Victorian stories, with Finley focusing on Reconstruction politics, along with race and class issues, after the Civil War. It is generally acknowledged that the series degenerated into travelogue, a popular genre in the late nineteenth century, and Elsie's extended family gets very large and too complicated to follow in later books in the series. Another travelogue series, Elizabeth W. Champney's Three Vassar Girls, is a forerunner of the high school and college series for teenage girls that followed at the turn of the century.

Jacob Abbott, who wrote a series of books about a boy named Rollo in the 1830s, is generally recognized as the creator of children's series books. Rollo's Cousin Lucy, who had appeared in Abbott's Rollo and Jonas boys' series books, got her very own girls' series in 1841. The Lucy Books featured "innocent adventures and mishaps, generously laced with moral and educational material."[4] The six books in the Lucy series, published in 1841 and 1842, were revised in the 1850s, and they were included on titles of recommended books for young readers for many decades. Abbott wrote several other girls' series in the latter half of the nineteenth century, including Mary Gay and Franconia. Abbott is also credited with the Americanization of children's literature.[5] Without Abbott's influence in children's literature during the nineteenth century, it is possible that American girls' series fiction might never have existed.

Other writers followed Abbott's lead and began to produce educational, moral, and religious series books for girls. Elizabeth Stuart Phelps, who had been a student of Abbott's, published a religious series of books about a girl named Kitty Brown between 1851 and 1853. By the 1860s, many new children's series had been introduced, but girls' series were mostly written for younger readers. Under the pen name Sophie May, author Rebecca Sophia Clarke wrote six series for primary grade readers, including Little Prudy, Flyaway, Dottie Dimple, and Flaxie Frizzle. Little Prudy was extremely popular, selling 300,000 copies by 1871.[6] May also wanted to write for teenage girls, and she eventually created the Quinnebasset series, published between 1871 and 1903, for the teen audience. Each book in the series featured a different girl growing up in Quinnebasset, Maine. Although May wanted to create more books for teen girls, poor health limited her writing.

The most popular and longest running girls' series of the nineteenth century is Elsie Dinsmore, whose life story is told in twenty-eight books published between 1867 and 1905. The first title alone sold nearly 300,000 copies in its first decade of publication, earning its author approximately a quarter of a million dollars, and *Elsie Dinsmore* went on to sell more than five million copies through the twentieth century.[7] The series, written by Martha Farquharson under the pen name Martha Finley, begins with eight-year-old Elsie living with her paternal grandparents and her father's siblings on an antebellum plantation called Roselands. Her mother is deceased, and her father has left her in the care of his family. Young Elsie is ostracized by her father's family, who never approved of her parents' marriage. She is taunted by her young aunts and uncles and abused by her step-grandmother and governess. Lonely Elsie is loved only by Aunt Chloe, her African American slave "mammy" who has raised her to be a good Christian girl, according to her beloved Mama's wishes. Elsie is happy for a short time when visitor Rose Allison, who is also a Christian, spends many hours reading the Bible with her, but Elsie longs for her father's love, and Horace Dinsmore finally returns to his family.

Young Elsie is confused by her father's coldness and strict rules. For instance, Elsie is not allowed to eat the same food as the other children in the household, because her father doesn't want her to eat things like butter and sugar. Elsie desperately wants to please her father because she thinks if she obeys him he will love her, so she tries to comply with his stringent rules. Even though the young Christian girl is portrayed as being better than everyone else in the household, she has her faults: "Elsie, though she possessed much of 'the ornament of a meek and quiet spirit,' was not yet perfect, and often had a fierce contest with her naturally quick temper."[8] This passage implies that Elsie needs to control her emotions to reach perfection. While Elsie tries to be the perfect Victorian child, her "father is the ultimate nineteenth-century patriarch," who tries to bully the emotional child into controlling her sentimental nature.[9]

When Horace punishes her unjustly several times, Elsie believes she must repent her sins, even though her young aunts and uncles are responsible for the various crimes for which she is punished. Elsie asserts herself, however, when her father wants her to sing a song to visitors on a Sunday. Even family friend Edward Travilla, who likes Elsie, tries to convince her that God won't be angry with her for singing and obeying her father's wishes. Elsie refuses and she is left seated at the piano, where she eventually faints, falls, and hits her head on the corner of a piece of furniture. When she regains consciousness, Elsie and her father reconcile. Scholar Deidre Johnson notes that Elsie "holds the position of being the only juvenile series heroine to die and be resurrected," and this happens several times in the first few books in the series.[10] When Horace asks if Elsie loves him more than anyone else, she replies, "No, papa, I love Jesus best. You next."[11] Horace is eventually converted to Elsie's Protestant Christianity in the second book, *Elsie's Holiday at Roselands*, but he only converts after another illness, brought on by a disagreement over her piousness and sentimentality, nearly kills young Elsie.

Horace begins to show his daughter much love and affection early in the series. In fact, the relationship between Elsie and her father appears to be incestuous, especially to more recent readers of the series. "Their relationship becomes even more disturbing because of its sexual overtones," with many kisses and caresses between father and daughter.[12] "I doubt if Mrs. Farquharson [Finley] ever suspected, but they *must* have been sleeping together," joked Hardy Boys ghostwriter Leslie McFarlane in his autobiography.[13] Perhaps later post-Freud readers are seeing something different than nineteenth-century readers saw in the father-daughter relationship, but the passionate talk and extensive touching between Elsie and Horace is disturbing. Although Horace marries Rose Allison in *Elsie's Girlhood*, he remains unusually close to his daughter. In *Elsie's Womanhood* she tells her fiancé, who is her father's friend and contemporary, Edward Travilla, that her father has been "father, mother, everything—but husband."[14] Elsie takes a replacement father for her husband, however, which is just as disturbing as her relationship with her father. Scholar Marla Harris argues the relationship between Elsie and her father can be "understood allegorically as that of a Christian and her God, or as that of a child and parent, or as wife and husband."[15] Perhaps Finley intended all three interpretations of the relationship, but joking aside, she probably did not intend for readers to regard it as incestuous.

Further complicating interpretations of the Elsie Dinsmore series, Harris suggests, "the language of ownership and possession that charac-

terizes Horace and Elsie's understanding of their relationship repro-
duces the language of master and slave."[16] Since the early books in the
series are set before, during, and after the Civil War, relationships between white Anglo-Saxon Protestant masters and African American
slaves permeate the books. While Elsie loves her Aunt Chloe, she actually owns the woman, but terms like "mammy," "servant," and
"housekeeper" are euphemistically used to describe the African Americans who work inside the family home.

Before her marriage to Edward Travilla in *Elsie's Womanhood*, Elsie
learns she is a very wealthy woman, having inherited from her mother
"several stores and a dwelling house in New Orleans, a fine plantation
with between two and three hundred slaves," and investments amount-
ing to three million dollars.[17] When Elsie and her father visit her plantation, Viamede, they arrive just in time to stop the whipping of a slave
woman. Elsie and her father ban cruel treatment of slaves on the plantation, and Elsie makes sure the slaves are properly housed, clothed,
and fed. During her stay, Elsie visits the slave quarters to conduct Bible
studies, and she hires a pastor to hold regular church services for them.
Elsie works to improve the living conditions of her slaves and help
them find salvation in death, rather than supporting the abolitionists
or helping her slaves escape North via the Underground Railroad.

By the time Elsie, Horace, and Aunt Chloe return home from Viamede, they have found Aunt Chloe's long-lost husband and granddaughter, and Elsie has purchased both slaves so Aunt Chloe, Uncle
Joe, and Aunt Dinah can be together. In fact, all of the slaves owned
by the Dinsmores and Travillas are so happy they stay with their former
owners even after they are freed in 1863. One doubts many former
slaves actually stayed with their former masters because they wanted to,
making this an unrealistic feature of the stories, although some freed
African Americans continued to work on plantations for wages. Finley
conveniently avoids much of the Civil War, sending the Dinsmores
and Travillas to Italy until the war is over, but some realities of life in
the postwar South are fairly accurately portrayed.

When Elsie and her family return to the United States, they find
homes and farms destroyed and many formerly wealthy plantation owners destitute. Horace's home and Elsie's fortune remain intact, but
Roselands and the Travilla family home are in ruins, and many family

members and friends have been lost in the war. Nevertheless, the Travillas and Dinsmores resolve to stay in the South, and they hire freed African Americans to work on their plantations for decent wages.

Elsie's Motherhood finds the Travillas and Dinsmores being persecuted by the Ku Klux Klan, a social organization founded in 1866 that sought to restore white supremacy by directing threats and violence toward freed African Americans. Ku Klux Klan members think Elsie's family is paying African American workers too much money for their work, so they harass them and threaten bodily harm. The focus of *Elsie's Motherhood* becomes class rather than race, with the former slaves happy with their situation and many white plantation owners very unhappy. Marla Harris argues, "Class conflict displaces race conflict for Finley as the impetus behind the Klan."[18] As a white woman writing about recent history, it is not surprising that she would focus more on class and gender issues, rather than racial politics. Finley's Reconstruction era story is really about conflict in the white upper classes, rather than a story about race conflict. Class conflict is present everywhere, including the Dinsmore family home, where everyone is financially dependent upon the wealthy, saintly Elsie.

Finley occasionally questions the dominant ideologies of class and gender and the connections between gender and class in the characters of Elsie's aunts Enna and Louise. Enna and Louise separate themselves socially from the rest of the family in *Elsie's Womanhood*, even though they are financially dependent on Elsie, after their father completely forgets them upon their brother's return from Italy. Enna snidely comments, "Daughters count for nothing; grandchildren are equally valuable. Sons, houses, and lands are the only possessions worth having!"[19] Although these cranky women point out gender and class inequities, they are clearly wrong for doing so, and pious Elsie seems even more perfect in comparison to her aunts.

Surprisingly, Finley does not shy away from contemporary politics, and critics have commended her for tackling postwar political affairs in *Elsie's Motherhood*. "The publication of the anti-Klan novel coincides with the highly turbulent moment when Reconstruction was coming to an end. I know of no other children's book writer who entered so boldly into the political debate of the era," contends children's literature expert Donnarae MacCann.[20] Nevertheless, Harris argues that Finley "stood at a psychic and geographical distance from her African American characters," limiting what she understood and wrote about during the period of Reconstruction after the Civil War.[21] This psychic distance has been a problem throughout the publishing history of girls' series fiction, most notable in the supremacy of white girls and the absence of girls of other races or ethnicities in the stories. Girls' series books, for both preteen and teen readers, remain largely the domain of such wealthy white girls as Elsie Dinsmore moving into the twenty-first century.

While Edward and Horace worry about protecting their families from the Ku Klux Klan, Elsie is busy caring for her children, Elsie, Edward, Violet, and Harold. Women were mothers in upper-class Victorian society, "'the angel in the house' who ministered to the spiritual and physical needs of the family."[22] Although Elsie is not as strict as her father, she still expects her children to behave properly and become good Christians. Scholar Pam Hardman suggests that Finley subverts the traditional Victorian domestic story by inviting men into the domestic sphere and allowing them to take control of women's space. Horace Dinsmore and Edward Travilla are able to move between male and female spheres, while Elsie remains confined to domesticity, with Finley challenging only traditional male gender roles. The Elsie Dinsmore series becomes a "Victorian tract" focusing on the blending of "spirituality and emotional intensity in an increasingly mechanical, industrialized society," and this takes place through the men in the story rather than the women.[23] Elsie is completely oblivious to the first wave of feminism, which emphasized the need for women's power in the public sphere through the suffrage movement and the domestic power of women as nurturers and submissive wives. Even Elsie's domestic power is taken away by the men in her life. Elsie is tamed by her father so she can be a submissive wife for her replacement father, and it is the compliant Elsie Dinsmore who is the model heroine for the hundreds of other girls' series protagonists that followed her.

Series book scholar Deidre Johnson recognizes Elsie Dinsmore's place in the history of girls' series books: "Elsie was one of earliest series heroines to come from an affluent, single-parent family and enjoy a close relationship with her father, a pattern most successfully repeated in the twentieth century with Nancy Drew."[24] Indeed, Elsie deserves to be recognized as "part of the series tradition of supergirls: multitalented females who have everything, do everything, and outshine everyone."[25] Johnson argues that Elsie's transformation from lonely girl to beloved supergirl was the nineteenth-century version of the Cinderella story, which was copied in other literary series, including Pollyanna and Anne of Green Gables. Vestiges of Elsie Dinsmore remain in girls' series fiction through the twenty-first century.

The Elsie Dinsmore series continued into the early twentieth century, following Elsie into old age and widowhood. Later books focus on Elsie's children and their extended families, and in the 1880s the books begin to resemble popular travelogues, with lengthy descriptions of travels and sightseeing. In the early twenty-first century, Christian publishers kept the original Elsie Dinsmore series, along with revised versions of the series, in print.

Elizabeth W. Champney's Three Vassar Girls series fit more neatly into the travelogue genre than the girls' series genre. Although Vassar connects the travelers, college life is not the focus of the stories. Champney, who was a member of Vassar College's first graduating class in 1869, sends students and graduates of her alma mater on exciting adventures around the world. Most of the books feature different girls and such different parts of the world as Europe, England, South America, and the Middle East. The series also contains numerous illustrations of popular tourist sights, many created by the author's artist husband, J. Wells Champney, who was known as "Champ."

In the last book in the series titled *Three Vassar Girls in the Holy Land*, published in 1892, Vassar student Violet Remington travels with her family and classmates Emma Constant and Bird Orchard to Alexandria, Egypt, where they begin a lengthy tour of the Holy Land, including Jerusalem, Bethlehem, and Beirut. During the trip, Bird falls in love with Violet's brother Frank, but Bird has a terrible secret. She is pretending to be a Christian girl; instead, she is really a "Jewess" named Zipporah Baumgarten. Coincidentally, Frank has already met Bird's parents on a previous trip to the Middle East, and he likes them very much. Like Martha Finley, Champney tackles the issue of American racism but with hope that it can be overcome.

Bird leaves the Remingtons to join her family in Jersusalem, believing that the Remingtons would never accept her or her family if they knew she was Jewish. But Bird must find them when she learns two new friends, including the man Violet loves, have been kidnapped for ransom. Bird spends several days traveling to catch up to the Remingtons, where she is accepted with forgiveness. Frank searches for Captain Blakeslee, and he learns that Bird's father has paid the ransom and rescued the Blakeslee. A double wedding, with Violet marrying Blakeslee and Bird marrying Frank, takes place "in a beautiful cedar grove on Mount Lebanon."[26]

Although two of the girls marry at the end of the story, all three Vassar girls have plans to do something productive with their studies when they graduate from Vassar. In fact, the trip to the Middle East is regarded as a learning opportunity for all three girls. Early in the story, Emma reflects on the Vassar girls' future plans:

> It was her ambition to take a special course in Hebrew and Old Testament literature such as is provided at Yale, and to fit herself thoroughly for Bible-class teaching of a high order. Violet was by nature an artist, and thought of such a tour as a wonderful sketching-field. Bird had a talent for literature, and would find a thousand themes for her graceful pen.[27]

Bird writes stories about the sights and history of the Holy Land, which she shares with her friends; Emma studies languages, and Violet and Frank recite poetry and sing songs throughout the book. Perhaps readers are meant to believe that Violet, who is an artist, drew the many pictures of historic buildings found throughout the book. Literary historian Shirley Marchalonis argues that, "the Vassar label . . . proclaims a privileged and separate status," and she suggests that these upper-class college girls have different opportunities than other girls.[28] The Three Vassar Girls series offers a contrast to Elsie Dinsmore, who fulfills her domestic and Christian duties rather than developing skills or talents of her own. Yet Elsie and all the girls in Champney's series are part of the privileged upper class, and it is the story of the nineteenth-century upper-class girl that sets the pattern for girls' series fiction.

Although the Three Vassar Girls series fit more neatly into the popular travelogue genre of the late nineteenth century rather than the girls' series genre, it is important because it foreshadows the college series that became popular with older girls in the early twentieth century.

"By the time the Elsie Dinsmore series ended in 1905, series fiction was well established as part of the reading diet of American children," argues series book scholar Deidre Johnson.[29] More series books for girls appeared in the late nineteenth century, and by the early twentieth century, series for teenage girls were coming into vogue with high school and college stories.

Notes

1. *The Oxford Companion to English Literature*, ed. Margaret Drabble, 5th ed., 2nd rev. (New York: Oxford University Press, 1998), 881.

2. Anne Scott McLeod, "From Rational to Romantic: The Children of Children's Literature in the Nineteenth Century," *Children's Literature*, 13.1 (1992): 141–53.

3. Pam Hardman, "The Steward of Her Soul: Elsie Dinsmore and the Training of a Victorian Child," *American Studies*, 29 (Fall 1988): 71.

4. Deidre Johnson, "From Abbott to Animorphs, from Godly Books to Goosebumps: The Nineteenth-Century Origins of Modern Series," *Scorned Literature: Essays on the History and Criticism of Popular Mass-Produced Fiction in America*, ed. Lydia Cushman Schurman and Deidre Johnson (Westport, CT: Greenwood, 2002), 149.

5. Jacque Roethler, "Abbott, Jacob," *The Oxford Encyclopedia of Children's Literature*, Vol. 1, ed. Jack Zipes (New York: Oxford University Press, 2006), 2.

6. Johnson, "From Abbott to Animorphs, from Godly Books to Goosebumps," 154.

7. Johnson, "From Abbott to Animorphs, from Godly Books to Goosebumps," 158.

8. Martha Finley, *Elsie Dinsmore* (1867; reprint, Nashville, TN: Cumberland House Publishing, 2000), 13.

9. Joanne Brown and Nancy St. Clair, *The Distant Mirror: Reflections on Young Adult Historical Fiction* (Lanham, MD: Scarecrow, 2006), 83.

10. Deidre Johnson, "Nancy Drew: A Modern Elsie Dinsmore?" *The Lion and the Unicorn*, 18 (1994): 15.

11. Finley, *Elsie Dinsmore*, 230.

12. Brown and St. Clair, *The Distant Mirror*, 83.

13. Leslie McFarlane, *Ghost of the Hardy Boys* (New York: Two Continents, 1976), 161.

14. Martha Finley, *Elsie's Womanhood* (1875; reprint, Nashville, TN: Cumberland House Publishing, 2000), 145.

15. Marla Harris, "A History Not Taught in Books: (Re)Writing Reconstruction in Historical Fiction for Children and Young Adults," *The Lion and the Unicorn*, 30.1 (2006): 100.

16. Harris, "A History Not Taught in Books," 100.

17. Finley, *Elsie's Womanhood*, 25.

18. Harris, "A History Not Taught in Books," 103.

19. Finley, *Elsie's Womanhood*, 341.

20. Donnarae MacCann, *White Supremacy in Children's Literature: Characterization of African Americans, 1830–1900* (New York: Garland, 1998), 163.

21. Harris, "A History Not Taught in Books," 113.

22. Patricia J. Campbell, *Sex Education Books for Young Adults, 1892–1979* (New York: R. R. Bowker, 1979), 17.

23. Hardman, "The Steward of Her Soul," 73.

24. Johnson, "From Abbott to Animorphs, from Godly Books to Goosebumps," 158.

25. Finley, *Elsie Dinsmore*, 230.

26. Elizabeth W. Champney, *Three Vassar Girls in the Holy Land* (Boston: Estes & Lauriat, 1892), 272.

27. Champney, *Three Vassar Girls in the Holy Land*, 20–21.

28. Shirley Marchalonis, *College Girls: A Century in Fiction* (New Brunswick, NJ: Rutgers University Press, 1995), 19.

29. Johnson, "From Abbott to Animorphs, from Godly Books to Goosebumps," 158.

2

𝕮𝕺

Schoolgirls and Sorority Sisters: Progressive Era High School and College Series

"After 1900, series fiction for American girls blossomed," notes series book expert Carol Billman.[1] Approximately ninety-four girls' series were published between 1910 and 1920, making it the "most productive period to date in terms of popular fiction for girls and female adolescents."[2] Girls' series often mixed several genres during this time period, as they moved further away from Victorian sentimental and religious stories, focusing instead on high school, college, sports, adventure, mystery, and the great outdoors. Literary historian Shirley Marchalonis argues:

> The nineteenth-century emphasis in women's fiction on the social, civilizing role of women and the specialized situation in which these traits flowered was apparently no longer enough to make a story. Girls began to have things happen: They solved mysteries, found long-lost children, and were even exposed to violence.[3]

Sentimental Victorian series, like Martha Finley's Elsie Dinsmore, continued to be popular. Although the series ended with *Elsie and Her Namesakes* in 1905, Finley's maudlin series has remained in print, and it is now considered classic girls' fiction. Edith Van Dyne's delightful Aunt Jane's Nieces series introduces three very different kinds of young heiresses. First published in 1906, Aunt Jane's Nieces is somewhere between a Horatio Alger "rags to riches" story from the 1890s and a girls' adventure series from the 1910s, making it transitional between girls' series genres.

School stories were also popular during the early twentieth century. Although college girls were first featured in Elizabeth W. Champney's Three Vassar Girls series in the nineteenth century, the series follows various Vassar girls on their travels around the world during school holidays. College girls first appeared at school in girls' series fiction in the early twentieth century, where they attended fictional women's colleges in the northeastern United States. Girls in series books "went to college in remarkable numbers . . . although less than 4 percent of American girls attended college in 1910, almost all the heroines in series fiction did."[4] But the years 1880 to 1910 are referred to as "the 'golden age' of the Northeastern women's college," so it is no surprise that many girls' series published during this time focus on women's college years.[5] Some series fiction followed girls from high school to college, while other series focused on just the high school or college experiences of women. Whether in high school or college, Progressive Era schoolgirls and college women are always white girls from the middle and upper classes.

"Between 1900 and World War I the old Victorian code [that] prescribed strict segregation of the sexes in separate spheres crumbled," argues historian Sara M. Evans.[6] Schoolgirls and college women are portrayed in a number of stereotypical contemporary roles, including the good Victorian girl, the all-around girl, the Gibson girl, and the athlete. The all-around girl is good at everything, while the glamorous Gibson girl, named for women in advertisements illustrated by artist Charles Dana Gibson, was fun, mildly athletic, and feminine. Very rarely are college girls and graduates in series fiction portrayed as the New Woman; the independent, college-educated career woman; the feminist suffragette; or the sexy flapper.

In 1903, author Amanda M. Douglas introduced Helen Grant, a very Victorian school and college girl who works as a teacher before she marries. Another Victorian series heroine introduced to readers in 1908, the Stratemeyer Syndicate's Dorothy Dale, is a good Christian girl whose life's mission is to help others become good, honest, and moral.

Margaret Warde's Betty Wales, who made her first appearance in 1904, is the perfect example of the all-around college girl. Warde was the first series fiction author to show readers what life was like in a women's college in her Betty Wales series, since Betty goes to college before Helen Grant. Other all-around college girls include Pauline Lester's Marjorie Dean and Nell Speed's Molly Brown. Only Grace Harlowe, first introduced in The High School Girls series in 1910, is portrayed in a variety of different roles of the Progressive Era New Woman. In 1920, shortly after World War I, Grace becomes an adventurer and athlete, driving an ambulance for the Red Cross in the Grace Harlow Overseas series and traveling around the United States on horseback in Grace Harlowe's Overland Riders series. Grace tries on all the socially acceptable roles for a New Woman of her class, skipping the more controversial roles of radical suffragette, sexy flapper, and independent career woman.

While Grace Harlowe and Marjorie Dean are portrayed as competent athletes, other series like the Stratemeyer Syndicate's The Girls of Central High and Edith Bancroft's Jane Allen, make female athletes the center of their stories. While The Girls of Central High participate in a wide range of team and recreational sports, Jane Allen is the star of the Wellington College basketball team.

Progressive Era high school and college series portrayed young women in a limited number of roles, focusing on the socially acceptable Victorian girl, the all-around girl, the Gibson girl, and the female athlete. High school and college girls are portrayed as being reluctant to give up the fun and freedom of their school days for marriage, even though they know marriage is a necessary part of life for grown women. Although protagonists in college series struggle with the idea of retiring to domestic life after college, virtually all of them get married. Series fiction made clear that the mission of women's colleges, first created in the 1860s, was to fully develop upper class women for their domestic roles as wives and mothers.

Victorian Girls

Although the Progressive Era began shortly before the turn of the century, good Victorian girls could still be found in girls' series fiction. The final four books in the long-running Elsie Dinsmore series were published between 1900 and 1905. These last books focus on Elsie's granddaughter, Lulu, and Elsie's large extended family. Mixed into these stories are lessons on religion, geography, and history. In the last book in the series, *Elsie and Her Namesakes*, Elsie's family simply returns home from a summer trip at the end of the story. *The Girls Series Companion* notes, "There is no cataclysmic finale such as we might expect from an epic series" like Elsie Dinsmore.[7]

Author L. Frank Baum, who published the popular book *The Wizard of Oz* in 1900, was invited by publisher Reilly & Britton to write a series for teenage girls called Aunt Jane's Nieces "in the style of Louisa M. Alcott stories, but not so good" in 1905.[8] Since Baum didn't want it known that he wrote books for teen girls, the female pseudonym Edith Van Dyne was created, and she was credited as the series author. According to his great-grandson, however, Baum had fun hinting about his authorship of the popular series. For example, the Baum's joined "Mrs. Van Dyne" for a meeting with a representative from another publisher, with Mrs. Van Dyne played by a female staff member of Reilly & Britton, or Maud Baum, depending on who was telling the story.[9] When Reilly & Britton launched another Edith Van Dyne series, *The Flying Girl*, Baum took out a newspaper advertisement that read, "Above is a picture of L. Frank Baum's home and gardens at Hollywood, California. In the center of the pergola is the little sheltered garden house where EDITH VAN DYNE, a guest of Mrs. Baum, wrote THE FLYING GIRL."[10] Baum amused himself by hinting about his pen name, daring someone to guess he was Edith Van Dyne.

It is clear that Baum loved writing the Aunt Jane's Nieces series as much as he enjoyed his female pseudonym. This entertaining series begins with three young cousins competing to inherit Aunt Jane's vast wealth, in a plot likely based on Shakespeare's play *King Lear*. Young, unsophisticated Beth DeGraf, glamorous debutante Louise Merrick, and fun, spirited Patsy Doyle visit Aunt Jane, who is on her deathbed. This clever story keeps readers guessing which girl is favored by the crabby old woman, and in the end, the fiery Patsy, who didn't want to inherit the money, seems to win the prize. But it turns out that Aunt Jane never owned anything to bequeath, and the relieved Patsy returns home to share the amusing adventure with her father. Long-lost Uncle

John Merrick accompanies her home, where he stays with the poor, generous Doyle family.

Although Uncle John appears to be a scruffy homeless man, he is really an eccentric billionaire who made his money in tin production and canning factories. Uncle John secretly arranges for a new apartment for the Doyles, a new job for Major Doyle, and a tutor to prepare Patsy for education at a women's college. As the first book in the series closes, Uncle John plans to financially support his other nieces, Beth and Louise. The series focuses on the nieces' travels in Europe, vacations on a farm, and society debuts. Louise marries Arthur Weldon in *Aunt Jane's Nieces in Society*, but they continue to spend time with her family. For fun, the girls sometimes take on work helping a cousin get elected to political office and running a newspaper. But it is clear the nieces are well cared for by Uncle John, and they work only when they want to, not because it is necessary. Many of the people, places, and adventures in the stories are actually based on Baum's own life. "The Baum family has always looked on the Aunt Jane's Nieces series as somewhat autobiographical of L. Frank's life," observed his great-grandson, Robert A. Baum.[11]

Although this might sound like a stuffy Victorian series about wealthy girls of leisure, it is actually well-written and highly entertaining, with many plot twists and fast pacing. All the characters in the series come to life, even the adults, and the books are wonderful to read. For a time, Baum's Aunt Jane's Nieces books sold more than even his Oz books, with the six titles in the Aunt Jane's Nieces series selling 22,569 copies in 1911.[12] "By the ninth book, the publishers were claiming that the series was one of the three best-selling girls' series in the world."[13] Baum learned from his publisher that the Aunt Jane's Nieces books "were particularly popular as gifts to girls graduating grammar school."[14] Baum took on the writing of several more series in 1911 to make more money, and biographer Katharine M. Rogers argues that all his series books, including *Aunt Jane's Nieces and Uncle John*, were "thin and flat" that year.[15]

Nevertheless, Aunt Jane's Nieces carried on until 1915, when Baum published *Aunt Jane's Nieces in the Red Cross*. In this story, Uncle John, his nieces, Patsy Doyle and Beth DeGraf, and their friend, Maud Stanton, go to Europe to work with the Red Cross during World War I. The girls nurse wounded soldiers of many nationalities for three months and then return home. Although Baum was supposed to write the new Mary Louise series for Reilly & Britton, he insisted on rewriting the ending of *Aunt Jane's Nieces in the Red Cross* first because the United States had joined World War I.

In the first edition of *Aunt Jane's Nieces in the Red Cross*, the girls express their admiration for all the soldiers, including the Germans. In the revised story, Baum sides "definitely with the Allies," and Uncle John decides to put all his money and energy into helping the Allies win the war.[16] Aunt Jane's nieces and their Uncle John remain in Europe, where Beth gets engaged to a French doctor who died in the original story, and Patsy's engagement is imminent when the series ends for the second time in 1918. A series that began as a Victorian farce and turned into a fun girls' adventure series ended on a very serious note. Books in the Aunt Jane's Nieces series remained in print until 1926.

Although schoolgirl Patsy Doyle is tutored at home in the Aunt Jane's Nieces series, some Victorian girls go to school and college in series fiction in the early twentieth century. Author Amanda M. Douglas introduced readers to a Victorian schoolgirl in *Helen Grant's Schooldays* in 1903. Helen wants to become a teacher, and several people help her, including her principal and a wealthy woman friend. After Helen's father dies in *Helen Grant's Friends*, she finishes high school and attends college. Although Douglas tried to portray college girl Helen as a modern woman, the "character remains the creation of a writer who lived most of her life in the nineteenth century."[17]

Even though Helen plans on teaching, Victorian notions of romance, marriage, domesticity, and womanliness dominate the series during Helen's college years. According to literary historian Shirley Marchalonis, "Helen Grant's college years are really an extended discussion of marriage."[18] In *Helen Grant, Senior*, the protagonist wonders, "Was a woman of many friendships capable of one strong, ardent affection for a person of the opposite sex, such as must constitute a well-ordered marriage?"[19] Although Helen turns down a marriage proposal while she is in college so she can finish her degree and go to work as a teacher, she finally gets engaged in *Helen's Grant's Decision*. The series came to an end in 1911 with *Helen Grant's Harvest Year*, presumably with Helen's marriage.

In 1908, Edward Stratemeyer introduced his first girls' series, Dorothy Dale, shortly after establishing his juvenile fiction factory known as the Stratemeyer Syndicate. Stratemeyer had worked as a ghostwriter of dime novels for publisher Street and Smith, and he followed the "rags to riches" formula of such popular dime novel writers as Horatio Alger and William Taylor Adams, who wrote under the pen name Oliver Optic. Just like publisher Street and Smith, Stratemeyer hired ghostwriters to write series books for boys and girls based on his drafted outlines. Using this method, he was able to produce more than fifty fiction series before his death in 1930. Stratemeyer first focused on tots' series like The Bobbsey Twins and such boys' adventure series as Dave Porter and The Motor Boys before he launched his first girls' series.

In Stratemeyer's first girls' series, Dorothy Dale, A Girl of To-Day, is a fourteen-year-old schoolgirl who vacillates between girlhood and adulthood. One minute she is a young girl sitting in her father's lap, the next she is surrogate mother to her younger brothers, breadwinner for the family during her father's illness, and moral compass for everyone in Dalton. Dorothy is already involved in the local temperance movement, promoting abstinence from alcohol. While it may seem strange for a young teenager to be involved in the temperance movement, the fact that it was led by the Woman's Christian Temperance Union suggests temperance work is a desirable activity for a young Christian woman. After all, the "most prominent women in Dalton were identified with the movement, and with such leaders surely no girl need be afraid to follow."[20] Major Dale praises his daughter for saving a man from alcoholism:

> Well, well, daughter, you were right in showing charity. Yes, charity is the love of God and our neighbor, and it was that love that led you to take the hand of that sick and discouraged man. Ralph told me how you brought him into the Bugle office that afternoon, and how that was the beginning of a new life to Burlock for he never tasted strong drink after that day.[21]

Major Dale suggests, however, that Dorothy work with a girls' fundraising auxiliary group instead of getting so closely involved with alcoholics. Her father allows her to help the reformed Miles Burlock find his missing wife and daughter. Even though Burlock dies early in the story, Dorothy continues searching for his family, and she eventually finds Burlock's young daughter, Nellie. In the rags to riches theme, Major Dale turns over the girl's inheritance, and he offers her foster father a job at his newspaper.

As an honorable and moral Victorian girl, Dorothy also acts as role model for her best friend, Tavia Travers, who is always getting into trouble. Dorothy's "common sense and ladylike qualities" are contrasted with Tavia's recklessness and irresponsibility.[22] Tavia's bad behavior is blamed on her mother, who is portrayed as a terrible homemaker and mother. So the motherless Dorothy, who has taken on the role of mother with her siblings, tries to help Tavia whenever she gets into mishaps. For instance, when a classmate blames Tavia for her sprained ankle, Tavia runs away, leaving Dorothy to cajole the girl into admitting that Tavia didn't cause her injury.

The real turning point for Tavia, however, comes when Dorothy recommends Tavia's father for the job of law enforcement officer in Dalton. The Travers family rises in society, and Tavia finally decides she wants to be a successful young woman, both academically and socially, to make her family proud. Tavia wants to be a successful student like her beloved friend, Dorothy, and the story ends with both girls passing the school year.

In *Dorothy Dale at Glenwood School*, an inheritance enables Dorothy to attend boarding school, where other girls are jealous of her. Dorothy continues to nurture people and solve the occasional mystery until 1924, when the series ends. By then, Dorothy is engaged to Garry Knapp, who has inherited his own fortune. In the final book in the series, *Dorothy Dale to the Rescue*, Dorothy uncovers a plot to ruin her fiancé's business. If the series had continued past Dorothy's marriage, she would likely have joined the Progressive Era women reformers, working in settlement houses for poor immigrant families founded by college graduates Jane Addams and Ellen Gates Starr in the late nineteenth century.

The ideals of Victorian domesticity, womanliness, and marriage still permeated girls' series fiction throughout the Progressive Era, even as new roles for middle and upper-class girls were possible. Girls from the lower classes, including immigrants, were not often found in girls' series books, unless they were scholarship students or maids.

The All-Around Girl and the
Gibson Girl in High School and College Series

In 1904, Smith College graduate Edith Kellogg Dunton published the Betty Wales college series, under the pen name Margaret Warde. *Betty Wales, Freshman* introduces readers to the Harding College all-around girl, her new friends, Helen Chase Adams and Eleanor Watson, and a whole group of girls who become known as the "Merry Hearts." While the girls in Amanda M. Douglas's Helen Grant series worry that college doesn't prepare them for marriage, the Betty Wales series focuses on college as a place to practice relationships, so the girls can become nurturing women before they get married.

In the first book in the series, caring Betty tries to help shy, studious Helen become more fun and outgoing. She also helps snobby Eleanor change her ways when she nearly fails all her courses. But the socially ambitious Eleanor needs Betty's help again in *Betty Wales, Sophomore*, when she is caught plagiarizing a short story from a literary magazine for a school assignment. It is Betty's job as the all-around girl to provide a role model for her classmates, and Betty accepts this job enthusiastically. Although Betty is a class leader, she is surprised when she is accepted into the Dramatic Club:

> "But to think the society wanted me!" said Betty in awestruck tones. "Helen, you know they never do take a person unless she amounts to something, now do they? But what in the world do I amount to?"
>
> "Does being an all-around girl count?" asked Helen. "Because the senior that is such a friend of Eleanor Watson's said you were that, and that's what you wanted to be, isn't it? But I think myself," she added shyly, "that your one talent that we used to talk about last year, you know, is being nice to everybody."[23]

While her friends and readers already know she is an all-around girl, Betty is the last to realize her strengths. According to scholar Sherrie Inness, "The all-around girl is the Progressive Era superwoman."[24] Although she doesn't excel at anything in particular, she succeeds at everything, including academics, school clubs, and sports. She is also a social success, making friends with everyone and hosting fabulous parties. Betty Wales is a likable character precisely because she doesn't realize she is an all-around girl. Literary historian Shirley Marchalonis argues that the focus on self-development in the Betty Wales series signals a change in fiction for girls' and women at the turn of the century: "The emphasis on the development of individual talents and strengths and the fulfillment of self . . . reverses the direction of so much nineteenth-century fiction by and about women."[25] Nevertheless, the all-around girl develops her talents to become the right kind of wife and mother in a middle-class or upper-class family, not to become an independent woman.

Although the stories emphasize personal development, Warde's series also portrays college as a time for women to bond in a segregated community of women. In the high school and college series of the early twentieth century, friendships between women are very affectionate, and crushes are often portrayed among friends. For instance, Eleanor Watson befriends young freshman Dora Carlson, and Dora develops a crush on her in *Betty Wales, Sophomore*. But rather than interpreting these friendships as veiled lesbian relationships, romances between women are merely portrayed as practice for their heterosexual lives with men after college.

Girl dances are common in the college stories, just as they were at the women's colleges in the early twentieth century, where sophomore girls invite freshman girls to a dance, send flowers, and escort their dates to and from the dance. "The behavior patterns connected with these dances act out both the masculine and feminine conventional courtship roles," reports Shirley Marchalonis.[26] In *Betty Wales, Sophomore*, Eleanor invites Dora to the sophomore dance early in the semester. Snobby Eleanor even tells her friends she likes Dora: "Dora Carlson is so absolutely frank and straightforward, and so competent and quick to see through things. She ought to have been a man."[27] Eleanor compares Dora to a man, so she doesn't mind the girl's crush. While her friends worry she will hurt Dora, Eleanor tells Betty she wants to be worthy of the girl's love and trust. Love and trust, however, are seen in the context of friendship, rather than sexual or physical love. Girl dances and affectionate female friendships are found in many of the high school and college girls' series of the Progessive Era, including Helen Grant, Molly Brown, Grace Harlowe, and Marjorie Dean. One girl whom readers suspect knows something about heterosexual relationships from experience, however, is Betty Wales's sophisticated friend, Madeline Ayres.

Madeline, first introduced in *Betty Wales, Sophomore*, is from Bohemia, New York. When Betty doesn't recognize the name of the city, Madeline replies, "Bohemia—the artistic New York. . . . It's very good fun, living in Bohemia."[28] While innocent Betty has never heard of Bohemia, the worldly Madeline comes from a turn-of-the-century community that included artists, socialists, and anarchist Emma Goldman, who publicly promoted free love and denounced marriage. Historian Sara M. Evans reports, "In the artistic and bohemian culture of New York's Greenwich Village . . . a community of 'sex radicals' proclaimed women's right to sexual pleasure and experimentation."[29] The Bohemians believed women should enjoy heterosexual sex within the marriage, and birth control advocate Margaret Sanger worked for the dissemination of contraceptives through doctors so married women could have sex without getting pregnant. In the character of Madeline Ayres, Warde makes a hidden reference to women's sexuality, which Betty completely misses. Innocent readers, like Betty, are simply thrilled to meet the intelligent, multilingual, well-traveled Madeline, who often seems omniscient.

In 1907, the Merry Hearts finish college, but the Betty Wales series continues to follow the girls' lives. While Madeline returns to Europe, another friend gets married, and many of the girls take jobs as teachers. Betty returns home to Cleveland. Since the quintessential college girl can no longer participate in such activities as sports and politics after she graduates from a women's college, "the all-around girl in college fiction is adrift."[30] Betty returns to Harding College to work as a financial aid secretary and student advisor for a short time in *Betty Wales on Campus*. She eventually marries Eleanor's brother, Jim Watson, in *Betty Wales Decides*, but before she marries, Betty and her friends grieve the loss of her independence. They all agree it is "the end of Betty Wales."[31] The girls recognize that marriage is a necessity rather than something they really want, and Betty finally gives in to necessity. Betty's marriage is not, however, the end of the series. The last two books in the series focus on Betty's friends and her career as a businesswoman until 1917.

In 1910, Josephine Chase published the first book in The High School Girls series under the pen name Jessie Graham Flower. The

High School Girls features the exciting adventures of Gibson girl Grace Harlowe and her friends at Oakdale High School. Stories focus on the antics of Grace and her friends Nora O'Malley, Anne Pierson, and Jessica Bright. Jealous classmates Miriam Nesbit and Eleanor Savell often cause trouble for Grace and her friends. In *Grace Harlowe's Junior Year at High School,* newcomer Eleanor is described as "reckless, self-willed, defiant of public opinion, and exceedingly impulsive," traits deemed by the middle and upper classes to be improper for a young woman, even during the Progressive Era.[32] Grace and her friends are asked to befriend Eleanor and "keep her out of mischief."[33] The girls invite Eleanor to join their sorority, but she doesn't want to spend time with good girls, and she forms a rival sorority. Nasty Eleanor disrupts a class performance of Shakespeare's play *As You Like It,* and afterward she tries to make amends by becoming friendly with everyone. After The High School Girls graduate, they go on to college.

In The College Girls series, Grace and her friends Anne Pierson and Miriam Nesbit attend Overton College. Grace becomes an all-around girl, meeting new friends, forming new clubs, and making new enemies jealous of her popularity. After Grace graduates from Overton, she returns to the campus to work as head of Harlowe House, a residence for underprivileged girls on campus.

Grace Harlowe author Josephine Chase also wrote the Marjorie Dean series, under the pen name Pauline Lester, following Marjorie's life from high school to college to postgraduate life working at Hamilton College.[34] Both the Grace Harlowe and Marjorie Dean series were "enormously popular" during the second and third decades of the twentieth century.[35] Shirley Marchalonis argues that both of Chase's heroines embody womanliness:

> Dainty Marjorie and tomboy Grace are exemplars and mother-figures, straightening out those who are heading in the wrong direction, solving problems for those in trouble, and consciously upholding a kind of semi-religious image of the college itself. And the message is clear: good triumphs, good women lead the way.[36]

Marchalonis suggests that Leslie Cairns, from the Marjorie Dean series, represents a contrast to the womanly Marjorie and Grace. She reports Leslie "is part of the 'roaring twenties,' the time of flaming youth, flappers, bobbed hair, and short skirts, with all the dramatic changes in women's behavior."[37] But this bad girl eventually comes around, modeling herself after Marjorie, becoming a womanly nurturer. Even though both Marjorie and Grace enjoy their work on campus, they are eventually ready for marriage. But Grace doesn't have an easy time deciding to marry Tom Gray. In *Grace Harlowe's Problem*, Grace must decide "whether she can shut love out of her life forever, just for the sake of her work."[38] Grace must decide whether to work or get married, implying that in the 1920s, a middle-class or upper-class woman couldn't have both a family and a career. But lower-class women did work outside the home. According to historian Sara M. Evans, "While the college-educated new woman and the youthful Gibson girl captured media interest, growing numbers of working women in blue-collar, clerical, and service occupations also reshaped the parameters of female experience."[39] Working women, however, were not the focus of girls' series fiction.

Grace may not work for a living, but after her marriage to Tom in *Grace Harlowe's Golden Summer*, she volunteers with the Red Cross and leads her friends across the country on horseback. Grace spends time working with the Red Cross in France, driving an ambulance during World War I. Shirley Marchalonis argues that Grace's war service reflects the reality of some women's lives during the war: "Women did take part in war work, driving ambulances, nursing, aiding refugees."[40] Before leaving France, Grace and Tom adopt a French girl named Yvonne. Grace Harlowe's Overland Riders series, published between 1921 and 1924, features the Western adventures of Grace, her husband, Tom, their daughter, and a group of friends. Through it all, Grace is portrayed as a "'womanly woman,' complete with a husband and child."[41] In the first book in this series, *Grace Harlowe's Overland Riders on the Great American Desert*, Elfreda Briggs asks her friend about her husband's reaction to her adventurous plans:

> "What I am curious about is how Tom ever came to consent to your attempting such an adventure."
> "I presume he really would have made serious objection had it not been for the fact that he had signed up for that forestry contract in Ore-

gon. Tom knew that I would have a lonely summer at home, and, I believe, deep down in his heart, felt that were he to deny me the pleasure of this trip, I might break my neck driving my car. You see, since I drove an ambulance in France I do not exactly creep along the roads with my spirited little roadster."[42]

When Tom joins the Overlanders later in the series, scholar Ellen Singleton argues, "it is a different Grace . . . who appears between the covers."[43] Grace goes from being an independent adventurer to the woman behind the adventurer husband, transforming into a domestic wife and mother. This may account for the series end in 1924, but *The Girls' Series Companion* notes that Grace Harlowe's Overland Riders series was "truly terrible," so this may be the real reason the series ended.[44]

It is interesting to note that the various series featuring Grace Harlowe, published between 1910 and 1924, shift and change to fit whichever subgenre of girls' series was most popular at the time. Moreover, the subgenres changed to match whichever image of young women was most socially acceptable. The series moves from schoolgirl and college stories to war and adventure tales, and with these changes, Grace goes from being a popular schoolgirl to an accomplished ambulance driver and horseback rider, and finally, to a submissive wife.

Nell Speed's Molly Brown college series, which began in 1912, struggles with the ideals of Victorian domesticity and women's new public roles in society. Perhaps this was because the series was actually written by two people, since Emma Speed Samson wrote the last half of the series after her sister's death. The Molly Brown series differs from other college series in its emphasis on heterosexual romance. Instead of girl crushes and girl dances, the girls at Wellington College focus their romantic energies on men. Although Professor Edwin Green falls in love with Molly at their first meeting in *Molly Brown's Freshman Days*, he waits until Molly graduates to confess his love for her. Although Molly doesn't think of Edwin as a lover or potential husband, he becomes her friend and confidante throughout her college days. Marchalonis suggests that, "the relationship is so typical of romantic fiction that the reader finds Molly's lack of awareness" difficult to understand.[45] A nearby men's college provides romantic interests for Molly's friends.

Molly and Edwin marry in 1915 after she graduates from college, but the series continues until 1921, focusing on the lives of Molly and her friends during World War I. In the last book in the series, *Molly Brown's College Friends*, Molly's friends discover German spies on campus during a class reunion. In complete contrast to Molly are the diverse group of people who are her friends at Wellington College, including a women's rights activist and a young Japanese woman, not found in other girls' series from the era. The series differs in additional ways from other girls' series published during the decade. *The Girls' Series Companion* notes that, "Lack of racial prejudice, emphasis on women's rights, and an effort to understand the German viewpoint in World War I are not often seen in juvenile series written prior to 1930," but all of these issues can be found in the Molly Brown series.[46]

High school and college girls in Progressive Era series fiction eventually all choose the domestic lives of wives and mothers, even though they had more fun and independence in school. Series fiction informs readers that they can have some measure of freedom, especially while in college, but it is women's duty to give up their own lives and become the nurturing member of a family. Within the middle-class and upper-class white world, according to girls' series fiction, women could not challenge the traditional Victorian notions of womanhood that prevailed. Sherrie A. Inness argues,

> College fiction . . . does not challenge the status quo of the outside world; instead, women's college graduates are trained to adjust themselves to their new situation and recognize that the college years must be only a fond memory for any woman who has successfully matured.[47]

Some real college-educated women, however, were busy challenging the status quo while these college series were popular. For example, female college graduates were involved with the mainstream National American Woman Suffrage Association and the more radical National Woman's Party, fighting for women's legal right to vote in national and local elections. But girls' series fiction only portrayed college girls in limited roles, including the good schoolgirl, the popular high school girl, and the successful college woman, and they were rarely portrayed as radical feminists, sexy flappers, or career women.

The Female Athlete in High School and College Series

The portrayal of female athletes in high school and college girls' series fiction shows some potential for carrying a subversive message about women's roles in society. Both Grace Harlowe and Marjorie Dean are physically active, playing basketball at school. Middle-class and upper-class women were able to participate in many different kinds of sports by the turn of the century, but the most popular sports at the women's colleges were gymnastics and basketball. Basketball, a game created in 1891 by physical education instructor James Naismith, was trendy at women's colleges during the Progressive Era.[48] This basketball trend is reflected in high school and college girls' series fiction. More women were becoming involved in athletics during the Progressive Era, encouraged by images of swimmer and movie star Annette Kellerman, whose swimming feats and movies promoted the idea that physical activity was a natural part of women's lives. "By the time these books were written, sports and athletics were well-established parts of college and high school," Shirley Marchalonis reports.[49] For a short time during the early part of the twentieth century, the female athlete was a role model for women.

Jane Allen, protagonist of Edith Bancroft's college series, plays basketball at Wellington College. She grew up a motherless tomboy on a Montana ranch, where she especially enjoys horseback riding. Jane has learned about college from a book series about fictional Beatrice Horton's life at Exley College, and she starts college life believing college girls are snobs. While her basketball skills are an asset, Jane realizes she "must learn to control her own pride, temper, and rebelliousness" if she wants to make friends and be successful at a women's college.[50] Jane has a difficult time adjusting to life in a women's community: "You see I've always lived in a man's world. Can you wonder that I don't care much for this world of girls I'm forced to live in?" Jane asks her new friend Judith.[51]

Before long, however, she is a popular leader of her class. "Janie is still the idol of the mob; anyone can see that, even at this early date," says her friend Ted at the beginning of *Jane Allen, Junior*.[52] Even without the help of a role model like Betty Wales, Grace Harlowe, or Marjorie Dean, Jane becomes a more "womanly woman" to fit into a community of women. In *Jane Allen: Senior*, Jane and Judith become social service workers in the tradition of Progressive female reformers, but since *Jane Allen: Graduate* was never published, we don't know anything about Jane's life after college. Very likely, Jane got married. It is clear, however, that in the last few books in the series, Jane moves away from the potentially subversive athlete role and closer to the ideal of the popular high school girl as she matures.

High school girls were also physically active during the last decade of the Progressive Era. In 1914, the Stratemeyer Syndicate launched The Girls of Central High, a series about a group of high school girls who participate in the Girls' Athletic Association. The Girls of Central High is unusual because it is "developed around the premise that girls can be highly physically active, and should play competitive interschool team sport."[53] Laura Belding, Bobby Hargrew, Nellie Agnew, Eva Sitz, Jess Morse, and twins Dora and Dorothy Lockwood participate in basketball, track and field, and rowing at school and in local competitions. Their coach, Mrs. Case, is portrayed as a typical girls' physical education instructor of the era, encouraging the girls to participate in many activities and promoting moderation in all things.[54]

Educator Ellen Singleton argues that The Girls of Central High is a unique girls' series because participation in sports is "essential to the character development of most of the girls in the group," instead of another inherent talent possessed by the already perfect protagonists.[55] Gertrude W. Morrison, the pseudonymous author of the series, reminds readers in each book, "The girls of Centerport had changed in character without a doubt since the three high schools of the city had become interested so deeply in girls' athletics."[56] The Girls of Central High spend some of their free time participating in such popular feminine activities of the era as helping the Red Cross and acting in amateur plays, but they also spend their leisure time skating, skiing, camping, playing hockey, swimming, hiking, boating, and riding horses. This unique series suggests, "Sports and sportsmanship make healthy, honorable girls who are on the way to becoming fine women."[57] The Girls of Central High series ended in 1921 with a book about the girls' work with the Red Cross, showing their talents for both social services and sports. If the series had continued, The Girls of Central High would likely have gone on to become wives and mothers who looked back fondly on their days as schoolgirls and athletes.

Girls' sports series ended around the same time the popularity of female athletics began to decline. Even the women's colleges that had endorsed competitive team sports in the prior decade stopped offering athletics to their students during the 1920s. "[M]any expressed fears that competitive athletics could make young women too masculine to be acceptable wives and, perhaps, even uninterested in marriage," historian Sara M. Evans contends.[58] Play days replaced competitive sports at women's colleges, and women's physical activities were once again limited.

While the domestic Victorian girl, the all-around girl, and the Gibson girl were all socially acceptable roles for women during the first three decades of the twentieth century, the female athlete was popular until the late 1920s, when she was banished from women's colleges and girls' series fiction. Only middle-class and upper-class society girls were portrayed in Progressive Era high school and college girls' series fiction. College girls always marry at the end of their series, even though some are reluctant, because the ideology of marriage and motherhood is supported in the series. The end of girlhood is usually marked by marriage at series' end.

Popular girls' series genres also included adventure and mystery between 1910 and 1930. The Stratemeyer Syndicate produced the two most popular girls' series in these genres, The Outdoor Girls and Ruth Fielding, securing their place as the top producer of girls' series books. Ruth Fielding changes from Victorian orphan, to all-around schoolgirl and college girl, to adventuresome Gibson girl, to career-oriented New Woman, wife, and mother during a span of more than twenty-one years, making Ruth the most complex girls' series heroine of the twentieth century.

Notes

1. Carol Billman, *The Secret of the Stratemeyer Syndicate* (New York: Ungar, 1986), 57.

2. Billman, *The Secret of the Stratemeyer Syndicate*, 57.

3. Shirley Marchalonis, *College Girls: A Century in Fiction* (New Brunswick, NJ: Rutgers University Press, 1995), 98.

4. Lucy Rollin, *Twentieth-Century Teen Culture by the Decades* (Westport, CT: Greenwood, 1999), 28.

5. Sherrie A. Inness, *Intimate Communities: Representation and Social Transformation in Women's College Fiction, 1895–1910* (Bowling Green, OH: Bowling Green State University Popular Press, 1995), 1.

6. Sara M. Evans, *Born for Liberty: A History of Women in America* (New York: Free Press Paperbacks, 1997), 160.

7. Society of Phantom Friends, *The Girls' Series Companion* (Rheem Valley, CA: SynSine, 1997), 150.

8. Katharine M. Rogers, *L. Frank Baum: Creator of Oz* (New York: St. Martin's, 2002), 135.

9. Robert A. Baum, "Aunt Jane's Nieces: An Introduction," in L. Frank Baum (writing as Edith Van Dyne), *Aunt Jane's Nieces* (Antioch, CA: The International Wizard of Oz Club, 2003), i–ii.

10. Baum, "Aunt Jane's Nieces," ix.

11. Baum, "Aunt Jane's Nieces," vi.

12. Rogers, *L. Frank Baum*, 184.

13. Baum, "Aunt Jane's Nieces," viii.

14. Rogers, *L. Frank Baum*, 186.

15. Rogers, *L. Frank Baum*, 187.

16. Rogers, *L. Frank Baum*, 219.

17. Marchalonis, *College Girls*, 95.

18. Marchalonis, *College Girls*, 143.

19. Amanda M. Douglas, *Helen Grant, Senior* (Boston: Lothrop, Lee, & Shepherd, 1907), 211.

20. Margaret Penrose, *Dorothy Dale, A Girl of To-day* (New York: Cupples & Leon, 1908), www.gutenberg.org (accessed January 23, 2007).

21. Penrose, *Dorothy Dale, A Girl of To-day*.

22. Deidre Johnson, *Edward Stratemeyer and the Stratemeyer Syndicate* (New York: Twayne, 1993), 112.

23. Margaret Warde, *Betty Wales, Sophomore* (Philadelphia, PA: Penn Publishing, 1905), www.gutenberg.org (accessed January 27, 2007).

24. Inness, *Intimate Communities*, 97.

25. Marchalonis, *College Girls*, 68.

26. Marchalonis, *College Girls*, 142.

27. Warde, *Betty Wales, Sophomore*.

28. Warde, *Betty Wales, Sophomore*.

29. Evans, *Born for Liberty*, 161–62.

30. Inness, *Intimate Communities*, 106.

31. Margaret Warde, *Betty Wales, Sophomore* (Philadelphia, PA: Penn Publishing, 1911), 355.

32. Jessie Graham Flower, *Grace Harlowe's Junior Year at High School* (Philadelphia, PA: Henry Altemus, 1911), www.gutenberg.org (accessed January 27, 2007).

33. Flower, *Grace Harlowe's Junior Year at High School.*

34. Kathleen Chamberlain, "Review of Shirley Marchalonis, *College Girls: A Century in Fiction*," H-PCAACA, H-Net Reviews, www.h-net.msu.edu/reviews/showrev.cgi?path=1508846635055 (accessed April 19, 2007).

35. Marchalonis, *College Girls*, 97.

36. Marchalonis, *College Girls*, 103.

37. Marchalonis, *College Girls*, 105.

38. Jessie Graham Flower, *Grace Harlowe's Problem* (Philadelphia, PA: Henry Altemus, 1916), 38.

39. Evans, *Born for Liberty*, 156.

40. Marchalonis, *College Girls*, 104.

41. Ellen Singleton, "Grace and Dorothy: Collisions of Femininity and Physical Activity in Two Early Twentieth-Century Book Series for Girls," *Children's Literature in Education*, 35.2 (2004): 124.

42. Jessie Graham Flower, *Grace Harlowe's Overland Riders on the Great American Desert* (Philadelphia, PA: Henry Altemus, 1921), www.gutenberg.org (accessed April 19, 2007).

43. Singleton, "Grace and Dorothy," 117.

44. Society of Phantom Friends, *The Girls' Series Companion*, 189.

45. Marchalonis, *College Girls*, 143.

46. Society of Phantom Friends, *The Girls' Series Companion*, 348.

47. Inness, *Intimate Communities*, 109.

48. Inness, *Intimate Communities*, 74.

49. Marchalonis, *College Girls*, 108.

50. Marchalonis, *College Girls*, 108.

51. Edith Bancroft, *Jane Allen of the Sub Team* (New York: Cupples & Leon, 1917), 266.

52. Edith Bancroft, *Jane Allen: Junior* (New York: Cupples & Leon, 1921), www.gutenberg.org (accessed January 27, 2007).

53. Ellen Singleton, "The Girls of Central High: How a Progressive Era Book Series for Girls Furthered the Cause of Female Interschool Sport," *Children's Literature in Education*, 37.3 (2006): 215.

54. Singleton, "The Girls of Central High," 217.

55. Singleton, "The Girls of Central High," 216.

56. Gertrude W. Morrison, *The Girls of Central High Aiding the Red Cross* (Akron, OH: Saalfield Publishing, 1919), www.gutenberg.org (accessed January 23, 2007).

57. Marchalonis, *College Girls*, 108.

58. Evans, *Born for Liberty*, 178.

3

❧

Adventure Girls and the New Woman: From the Progressive Era to the Jazz Generation

Although school and college stories were very popular during the early twentieth century, they were not the only kinds of girls' series available. Adventure stories, based on similar boys' series and focusing on such new technologies as motorcars, planes, and moving pictures were most popular between 1910 and 1920. Stories featuring automobile adventures were especially trendy since more people, including teens, could afford motorcars when Henry Ford's Model T was introduced in 1908 for $850.[1] A few years after their upper-class male counterparts had fun motoring in groups, The Automobile Girls, The Motor Girls, and The Motor Maids found many adventures riding around in their new motorcars. According to literary historian Nancy Tillman Romalov, "the automobile became both a symbolic and an actual source of independence for women."[2] Other adventure series, like The Girl Aviators and The Girl Flyers, featured female aviatrixes, while the Girl Scouts and Camp Fire Girls series featured skilled campers and homemakers. The Stratemeyer Syndicate's The Outdoor Girls, who seek adventures hiking, boating, and motoring, were the most popular adventure girls.

Mystery was always an element of these adventure stories, but the mystery genre became more important during the 1920s, when mystery stories became popular with American readers. The Stratemeyer

Syndicate worked to perfect the mystery genre with its Ruth Fielding series. Although the series began as an orphan and boarding school collection, it quickly included adventure, college, career, and mystery stories, and by the 1920s mystery was the most significant element in the series. Ruth is portrayed as a poor orphan, all-around school and college girl, skilled writer, superb actress, savvy businesswoman, brave adventurer, smart detective, and loving wife and mother, making her the ultimate New Woman in girls' series fiction. Although the Ruth Fielding series is unique for mixing so many different women's roles and genres, ultimately these many genres conflicted, and the series began losing its audience in the late 1920s. When Ruth Fielding's star began to fade, Edward Stratemeyer focused on creating several new girl detectives, including Betty Gordon, Billie Bradley, and Nancy Drew.

Adventure Girls

In 1910, the first girls' adventure series were published, including The Automobile Girls, featuring sisters Bab and Mollie Thurston, their friends Ruth Stuart and Grace Carter, and chaperone Aunt Sallie Stuart. Wealthy Ruth befriends the poor Thurston girls when she spends the summer in their hometown of Kingsbridge, and the girls use Ruth's car to catch a thief in *The Automobile Girls at Newport*. The Automobile Girls travel all over the United States in Ruth's car, including the Berkshires, Sleepy Hollow, Chicago, and Florida, and along the way they fight fires, find missing children, and locate buried treasure. In the last book in the series, titled *The Automobile Girls at Washington*, the famous quartet visits Ruth's cousin, Harriet Hamlin, in Washington, D.C. In a conversation with a female journalist interested in doing a newspaper story about The Automobile Girls, Bab states:

> For the past two years, since I have known Ruth Stuart, the "Automobile Girls" have traveled about in this country a good deal. But we are only school girls still. We have never really made our debut in society, although we mean to forget this while we are in Washington, and to see as much of the world as we can.[3]

The girls meet American and foreign diplomats at parties in Washington, and they even attend a reception at the White House, where they meet the president of the United States. When Bab discovers her sister Mollie borrowed money from Harriet to buy a dress for the White House reception, she seeks help from society matron Mrs. Wilson, rather than ask her friends for money. In return, Mrs. Wilson asks her to play a joke on Mr. Hamlin by stealing documents from his office, but Bab refuses. Mrs. Wilson finds a willing thief in Harriet, who is in debt to her dressmaker. By this time, Harriet has already asked her friend, Charlie Meyers, for money and refused it when he offers the money with the condition that she marries him. Harriet rejects the marriage proposal, stating, "But please remember that my affection is something that mere money cannot buy."[4]

Harriet makes a deal with Mrs. Wilson for money in return for papers from her father's office. When Bab and Ruth realize Harriet is desperate enough for money to betray her father and her country, they intercept the papers and replace them with blank sheets before they are delivered to Mrs. Wilson. But Harriet runs away to marry Charlie before she knows Bab and Ruth have saved her reputation. Fortunately, Charlie refuses to marry Harriet, who is welcomed back home. Spies Mrs. Wilson and her accomplice disappear from Washington society, and the girls are invited to a private meeting with the president, who thanks them for their service to their country. "It was a pretty trick you played on our enemies. Strategy is sometimes better than war, and a woman's wits than a man's fists," the president tells the girls.[5] After their second visit to the White House, Mr. Stuart arrives to take The Automobile Girls home. The series ends on a high note, when the girls learn Mr. Stuart and Mrs. Thurston will marry, making best friends Bab and Ruth sisters. In another similar series, The Motor Maids, the girls travel abroad to England and Japan.

Edward Stratemeyer's The Motor Girls followed the success of The Motor Boys, and the series began publishing in 1910. Author Margaret Penrose was "an expert automobilist," according to series advertisements. In fact, Penrose was a Stratemeyer Syndicate house name, and the books were likely written by ghostwriter Lillian Garis. When *The Motor Girls* opens, seventeen-year-old Cora Kimball is looking at her new motorcar, and she can't wait to learn how to drive it. Cora nicknames her car The Whirlwind, and before long, she is driving around the countryside accompanied by her best friends, twins Bess and Belle

Robinson. The girls get involved in an adventure when a wealthy friend loses a wallet containing a large amount of money and the empty wallet is discovered in Cora's car. The Motor Girls find their friend's money, and by the end of the first book in the series, Bess and Belle have their own motorcar. The Motor Girls continue their adventures until 1917, traveling around the United States and helping people who need them. Other girls' adventure series featured young female airplane pilots, for example The Girl Aviators and The Girl Flyers.

The most popular girls' adventure series was the Stratemeyer Syndicate's The Outdoor Girls, written by ghostwriters under the pen name Laura Lee Hope, the pseudonymous author of the popular juvenile series The Bobbsey Twins. In *The Outdoor Girls of Deepdale*, published in 1913, readers meet group leader Betty Nelson, shy and timid Amy Stonington-Blackford, outgoing Mollie Billette, and beautiful Grace Ford, who is a fashionable Gibson girl. When these middle-class and upper-class girls aren't busy with their adventures, they are girls of leisure, sitting around on lazy summer days eating chocolates and drinking lemonade.

The Outdoor Girls plan a summer walking tour, but before they leave, they find a $500 bill. The girls leave the money with Betty's father and go on their trip, where small adventures include helping a lost child find her way home, feeding a hungry tramp, and finding a deserted house. Of course, these girls of leisure stop with family and friends overnight, and their trunks are shipped ahead of them so they have all the comforts of home everywhere they go. During their travels, they learn about a man on a train who has lost money, and they wonder if this man lost a $500 bill. They finally find the man when he jumps off a train trestle to escape death, and it turns out to be Henry Blackford, whom they met earlier disguised as a hungry tramp. After the girls return to Deepdale, Blackford is very grateful when they restore his fortune.

While The Outdoor Girls are walking around the countryside, they are often mistaken for suffragettes, or women activists who sought legal voting rights for women. When a child cries out, "Mama! Come see the suffragists!" Betty responds, "Oh, mercy! . . . What will we be taken for next?"[6] Later the same day a woman asks, "What be you—suffragists?" went on the woman, with a smile. "That's the second time we've been taken for them today," murmured Betty. "Do we look so militant?"[7]

The Outdoor Girls are horrified to be mistaken for suffragists. "It is not surprising that these assertive, independent young women who insist on traveling only in the company of females should be taken for suffragettes, a catch-all term for emancipated women of the early part of the century," argues literary historian Nancy Tillman Romalov.[8] But it is implied suffragettes are bad girls, and the healthy young heroines don't want to be associated with such people. Even so, the girls adopt language used by suffragists. When someone mentions they are on a hike, Betty doesn't understand what the word "hike" means; Mollie explains, "Suffragist lingo for walk."[9]

The Outdoor Girls appear to be liberated, even if they don't want to be mistaken for suffragists. "They didn't wear bustles, or look generally helpless, and they could set out in their cars to do whatever they had the notion to do," notes Bobbie Ann Mason, but the "girls weren't truly independent, for their money came from Daddy and their main interest was boys."[10] The Outdoor Girls and their sister adventurers The Automobile Girls, The Motor Girls, The Meadow-Brook Girls, The Blue-Grass Seminary Girls, The Girl Aviators, and The Girl Flyers had more independence than many women, however, because they could afford to drive cars and fly planes.

The Outdoor Girls have many adventures and solve a few mysteries while they vacation at lakes, camps, beaches, and islands. "These girls, like their male counterparts, led the 'strenuous life' advocated by Teddy Roosevelt," reports teen culture historian Lucy Rollin.[11] The girls work hard for a short time in two books set during World War I, *The Outdoor Girls in Army Service* and *The Outdoor Girls at Hostess House*, when they join the Red Cross and open a Hostess House. During the war, the Young Women's Christian Association established and staffed Hostess Houses, guided by Vera Charlotte Scott Cushman, near military bases, hospitals, and ports to house women involved in war work. Nurses, Signal Corps workers, and Red Cross volunteers all stayed in Hostess Houses during the war.[12] Even though The Outdoor Girls are busy helping with the war effort at home, they find time to help an old woman search for her missing son and share some romance with their boyfriends before they ship out.

After the war, The Outdoor Girls continue their adventures on farms, on ranches, in the mountains, in Cape Cod, and at many other exciting locales. Whenever they have to catch thieves, gypsies, or imaginary monsters, their boyfriends come to their rescue. Although The Outdoor Girls have boyfriends, their romances are light and innocent, and they certainly don't participate in the group petting parties popular with teens in the 1920s. In the fantasy world of girls' series books, teenage girls are not sexual beings, even though women's sexuality was finally acceptable within the context of marriage. Birth control, promoted in the United States by Margaret Sanger during the early decades of the twentieth century, was not needed in this fantasy world. Just as in real life, the long-term goal of a well-to-do adventure girl is to make a good marriage. Through the second half of the 1920s, as the original Outdoor Girls marry, new girls join the group, including Irene Moore, Stella Sibley, Carolyn Cooper, and Meg and Lota Bronson. Nevertheless, The Outdoor Girls series remained popular, selling $1 million worth of books in 1922.[13]

During the 1920s, American society reacted to women's sexual and political liberation with a new emphasis on domesticity and marriage. As the traditional goal of marriage was reinforced and young women competed for male attention, bonds formed amongst females in college and service organizations broke easily. By the late 1920s, girls' series fiction publishers and authors noted this trend and shifted from writing about groups of girls to the adventures of one special girl who was not yet ready for romance and marriage. Adventure stories were replaced with mystery series featuring a single girl detective in the 1920s and 1930s. The Outdoor Girls lasted longer than most other girls' adventure series, but it was finally cancelled in 1933.

While it seems on the surface that adventure girls are independent because they have a car or a plane, they are actually dependent on their wealthy parents for their freedom, leisure, and money. Some of the girls are even dependent on the kindness of their friends, like Bab and Mollie Thurston, since their own families are not wealthy. Some of the groups, like The Automobile Girls, are chaperoned by adults everywhere they go. So while they have a measure of independence, adventure girls are not truly free of the constraints of their upper-class society, no matter how far their cars will take them or how high their planes will fly. Literary historian Ilana Nash notes, "While these hiking, driving, and flying heroines covered many miles geographically, they advanced only a few feet ideologically."[14]

Another kind of adventure series featured female campers. In 1912, Juliette Low founded the Girl Scouts of America, and Dr. Luther Gulik and his wife, Charlotte, founded the Camp Fire Girls. Both organizations focused on teaching girls about women's domestic and nurturing roles in society. Shortly after these organizations were founded, publishers launched Girl Scouts and Camp Fire Girls series books, even though the series were not endorsed by the organizations. The Girl Scouts and Camp Fire Girls series books promoted domesticity, femininity, and heterosexual romantic love. Scholar Ellen Singleton reports, "Girls went to camp to learn to keep house. If they did not want to be homemakers, they went to camp to learn why they should."[15] Girls in the stories learn such domestic skills as cooking and basic nursing care, even while they are camping.

While groups of girls experienced fun and adventures camping with their friends in the Girl Scouts and Camp Fire Girls series, they were constantly reminded of their womanly duties to society. For instance, in Margaret Vandercook's *The Camp Fire Girls at Sunrise Hill*, Esther Clark recites the Law of the Camp Fire for a group of girls before they go to camp: "Seek beauty. Give service. Pursue knowledge. Be trustworthy. Hold on to health. Glorify work. Be happy."[16] The girls discuss the difficulties of living up to such laws, but they are determined to try because they believe it is the key to happiness. Happiness means being successful in romantic love, and the girls believe the key to finding romantic love is in the Law of the Camp Fire. "Romantic love and a life lived happily ever after were the incentives held out to 'womanly' females, and innumerable examples were presented in these stories to young readers," argues Singleton.[17]

While the adventure series featuring such technological toys as motorcars and airplanes encouraged girls to dream of independence and action, camping stories encouraged girls to dream of domesticity, marriage, and love. Although girls' adventure series were published at the same time as the first feminist movement in the United States, none of these series promotes women's economic, political, or sexual freedoms. Instead, the books promote such "womanly" activities as driving, feminine sports, leisurely vacations, and domestic duties, mostly among an elite group of teen girls. Literary historian Nancy Tillman Romalov concludes:

> Having set their heroines up with the ability, courage, independence, and athleticism required to enact heroic adventures that the genre calls for, the authors then set about negating, disrupting, or dismissing the radical possibilities that might have been realized.[18]

The New Woman: Ruth Fielding and Her Sister Sleuths

Created during the most productive time in the Stratemeyer Syndicate's history, the Ruth Fielding series was launched in 1913. In the tradition of L. M. Montgomery's popular novel *Anne of Green Gables*, orphan Ruth Fielding moves to the Red Mill to live with her miserly old Uncle Jabez in *Ruth Fielding of the Red Mill*. Ruth becomes friends with well-to-do twins Helen and Tom Cameron, who both like Ruth very much, and she becomes "the preeminent 'charity child' on the go."[19] When Ruth, Helen, and Tom rush around in the Cameron's motorcar to warn everyone the dam has broken, they arrive at the Red Mill just in time to see Uncle Jabez's office disappear, along with his cashbox. The story quickly involves mystery when Ruth discovers that evil Jasper Parloe actually stole the money, and she gets her uncle's money back. Stingy Uncle Jabez decides he will pay for Ruth to attend Helen's boarding school, symbolizing the impact of Ruth's goodness and innocence on a mean old man. The books quickly move from an orphan story to a boarding school series, when Ruth and Helen go away to school in *Ruth Fielding at Briarwood Hall*.

At Briarwood Hall, Ruth and Helen get caught between two girls' clubs. While Helen joins the Upedes club, Ruth decides she doesn't like either club recruiting her, so she forms her own club for new students called Sweetbriars. Helen eventually realizes she was wrong to join another group. Ruth discovers the mystery of the ghostly campus harpist, and she learns he is the French teacher's brother, who is harassing his sister for money. While the early books focus on Ruth's school and college days up until World War I, it becomes clear very early in the series that Ruth will also be a career woman and a detective. Ruth becomes the ultimate New Woman, being college educated, unmarried, and financially independent. Stratemeyer Syndicate historian Carol Billman notes the importance of Ruth Fielding:

> She is one of the best representatives of her many contemporary series heroines—best because of her series popularity and because of her own position as a pivotal figure in fiction for American girls. Ruth is the orphan, a carryover from the nineteenth century sentimental tradition, turned movie star and sleuth, two new roles for fictional heroines of the 1900s."[20]

In 1916, Ruth becomes a "scenario" writer of silent moving pictures, a growing industry during the first two decades of the twentieth century, after a chance encounter with a film crew in *Ruth Fielding in Moving Pictures*. When Ruth, Helen, and Tom rescue actress Hazel Gray from a river, Alectrion Film Corporation head Mr. Hammond decides that he likes Ruth, and he promises to read her film scenario. In a scene resembling a sexual flirtation, Ruth is both innocent and aggressive:

> "Oh, Mr. Hammond!" gasped Ruth, with clasped hands. "Will you really *read* it?"
>
> "Of course I will," laughed the gentleman. "No matter how bad it is. That's a promise. Here is my card with my private address upon it. You send it directly to me, and the first time I am at home I will get it and give it my best attention. That's a promise," he repeated.
>
> "Oh, thank you, sir!" murmured Ruth delightedly, smiling and dimpling.
>
> He pinched her cheek and his eyes grew serious for a moment. "I once knew a girl much like you, Miss Ruth," he said. "Just as full of life and enthusiasm. You are a tonic for old fogies like me."
>
> "Old fogy!" repeated Ruth. "Why, I'm sure you're not old, Mr. Hammond."
>
> "Never mind flattering me," he broke in, with assumed sternness. "Haven't I already promised to read your scenario?"
>
> "Yes, sir," said Ruth, demurely. "But you haven't promised to produce it."[21]

Mr. Hammond is so impressed with her work and enamored with the girl that he agrees to film her movie to raise money for Briarwood Hall.

Mr. Hammond asks to see everything Ruth writes in the future for possible film production, opening up a career path for Ruth that leads to her financial independence at a very young age. Another Stratemeyer Syndicate series from the decade, The Moving Picture Girls, features teen sisters who are members of the Comet Film Company. Despite the popularity of the movies, The Moving Picture Girls were not as popular as Ruth Fielding, and the series was cancelled in 1916.

Ruth and Helen attend Ardmore College after graduation from high school, where Ruth is already known for her film work. When the United States joins World War I in 1917, they return home to work for the Red Cross. Ruth uses her scenario writing skills to make a movie about the Red Cross to encourage contributions. While Ruth and Helen work for the Red Cross, Helen's twin brother, Tom, enlists in the army. A conversation between Ruth and Helen informs readers about their different views on the roles of men and women in society. Referring to Tom, Ruth states:

> "But he is a man now. There is a difference in the sexes in their attitude [toward] this war which should establish in our minds that we are not equal."
>
> "Who aren't equal?" demanded Helen, almost wrathfully, for she was a militant feminist.
>
> "Men and women are not equal, dear. And they never will be. Wearing mannish clothes and doing mannish labor will never give women the same outlook upon life that men have. And when men encourage us to believe that our minds are the same as theirs, they do it almost always for their own selfish ends—or because there is something feminine about their minds."
>
> "Traitor!" cried Helen.
>
> "No," sighed Ruth. "Only honesty."[22]

This passage is interesting because it refers to Helen as a "militant feminist," which is still used as a derogatory phrase used to describe feminists. During the decade in which this story was written, feminist activists sought both the vote for women and world peace, as a Great War seemed likely. Carrie Chapman Catt, president of the National American Woman Suffrage Association, and Jane Addams, founder of the Women's Peace Party and the settlement house movement, actively opposed World War I. If Helen Cameron was really a militant feminist, she would be involved with the suffrage movement or the Women's Peace Party, not the Red Cross. W. Bert Foster, the Stratemeyer Syndicate ghostwriter for early books in the Ruth Fielding series, merely makes Helen a militant feminist for a moment to let readers know Ruth's stand on women's roles in society. Surprisingly, Ruth believes men and women have innately different talents, and she supports separate spheres for the sexes. Later in the story, however, career and college woman Ruth continues to break down the barriers to the public male sphere when she travels to France to work for the Red Cross during World War I.

Ruth works at hospitals in Lyse and Clair, organizing Red Cross supplies and helping soldiers write letters to their families. She also helps police capture thieves stealing supplies from the Red Cross, experiencing bombings and gunfire the whole time. She finally sees soldier Tom Cameron at the end of the story, and a future romance seems likely. In a most extraordinary girls' series book set during World War I, Ruth and a French soldier successfully cross No Man's Land into German camps to rescue Tom in *Ruth Fielding at the War Front*. Instead of staying home, Ruth travels "over there," landing right in the middle of the action. Another series that portrayed young women on the front lines of World War I is Margaret Vandercook's The Red Cross Girls. In this series, nurses Sonya Valesky, Bianca Zoli, Nona Davis, and Mildred Thornton work with the Red Cross in Britain, France, Belgium, Russia, and Italy. But even these Red Cross nurses don't get as close to the military action as Ruth Fielding.

Before the war is over, Ruth is sent home after she is injured in a bombing. *Ruth Fielding Homeward Bound* tells the story of her harrowing trip home, when everyone constantly worries about being attacked by German U-Boats. German pirates capture Ruth's ship, and the passengers and crew are held hostage. In an unrealistic air accident, Tom Cameron ends up on a German Zeppelin airship, which he crashes into the ocean near Ruth's ship. He is rescued by the pirates, who think he is German, and Tom bides his time until he can rescue Ruth and the other hostages.

Ruth spends the decade after World War I working as a film writer and actress for the Alectrion Film Corporation. Ruth's glamorous lifestyle may have been appealing to young readers, but she is portrayed as a "no-nonsense, unsentimental, independent, aggressive, ambitious, and assertive" career woman.[23] In fact, Ruth had much in common with popular actress Mary Pickford, her contemporary who was "a canny and hardworking businesswoman."[24]

By the 1920s, a new form of courtship called dating allowed young people to go out without chaperones, but Ruth and Tom don't really date. Instead, they are good friends who have a light romance. Tom Cameron proposes marriage in *Ruth Fielding in the Great Northwest*, but Ruth wants a career and her own life. "While she is no flapper, Ruth Fielding is a thoroughly contemporary heroine. Among the au courant pastimes Ruth engages in (beyond the films and automobiling) are airplane piloting and swimming," argues Billman.[25] While Stratemeyer didn't allow Ruth to become a sexy flapper, like such actresses as Clara Bow and Joan Crawford, she is an active young woman with many exciting interests.

Ghostwriter Mildred Wirt, a graduate student at the University of Iowa, was hired in the late 1920s to write the Ruth Fielding series. Wirt was a good choice for ghostwriter for the Ruth Fielding series because she was a modern woman who shared Ruth's interests in writing, swimming, and flying. Wirt took over the series at a time when Ruth's love life became more important, and Ruth finally agrees to marry Tom in *Ruth Fielding at Cameron Hall* in 1928. "Surprisingly, the series does not end there," notes Deidre Johnson.[26]

Instead of becoming a homemaker after her marriage, like other fictional women's college graduates, Ruth continues to work and solve mysteries. Although Tom is supportive of Ruth's career, she still struggles with her dual roles as wife and career woman, just like her ghostwriter. Wirt was able to write about these issues easily, since she was both a married woman and journalist. According to biographer Melanie Rehak, Wirt wanted to maintain some independence after she married. "Her intentions ran absolutely counter to what America expected of its young women at the end of the 1920s," just like Ruth's plans.[27] Even after Ruth and Tom have a baby, she continues to work. But she is "conflicted regarding her right social roles and her relationships with those around her" after her marriage, something she didn't worry about before she married.[28]

Ruth continues to work, and as the mystery genre becomes more central to the plots, she solves mysteries related to her work in the film industry. While the mystery genre was always present in this complex series, mysteries became more important as the series developed. Ruth catches kidnappers, imposters, and thieves. Despite the popularity of mysteries, Ruth Fielding's many roles as detective, wife, mother, and career woman brought "irreconcilable structural—actually, genre—differences" to the series that could not be sorted out, bringing an end to the collection in 1934.[29] The final book ends with Ruth declaring, "I'm home never more to roam. . . . If there are any more adventures in our little family, they will be passed on to June."[30] Ruth Fielding was the first full-fledged Stratemeyer Syndicate girl detective, and even though she was famous, her fame would ultimately be eclipsed by another, more popular Syndicate girl detective, Nancy Drew. But the Stratemeyer Syndicate had to perfect the girl detective formula before Nancy Drew could be created.

In 1920, the Stratemeyer Syndicate introduced another orphan girl detective, Betty Gordon. "Betty Gordon . . . seems an attempt to repeat Ruth Fielding's success but marks a shift toward emphasizing the protagonist's girlhood," suggests Stratemeyer Syndicate historian Deidre Johnson.[31] When the series opens, Betty is spending the summer with farmer Joseph Peabody, "a domineering, pitiless miser," his wife Agatha, "a drab woman crushed in spirit," and young Bob Henderson, "a poorhouse rat" who works at Bramble Farm.[32] Betty's uncle, a wealthy businessman who frequently travels, arranges for her to stay at the Peabody's farm. But he doesn't know Betty is abused by the mean farmer.

Betty runs away from Bramble Farm, in the hopes of finding her uncle in Washington, and instead she is intercepted by the kind Littel family. Although the wealthy Littels first mistake Betty for their cousin, the family likes her, so they take care of her while she waits for word from her uncle. Betty finds Bob in Washington, and she solves the mystery of the missing land deed Bob is accused of stealing from Bramble Farm. Betty and Bob travel to Oklahoma, where Uncle Dick adopts Bob.

Betty spends the rest of the series solving mysteries at Shadyside School, and she enjoys holidays with cousins Libbie and Bobby Littel. "Betty's closest female friends, Libbie and Bobby Littel, are the prototypes for Nancy Drew's friends, Bess Marvin and George Fayne. Overweight Libbie is a dreamy romantic who is teased by boyish Bobby."[33]

The Betty Gordon series attempts to copy the formula used in the popular Ruth Fielding series, and at the same time, is also a forerunner of the Nancy Drew Mystery Stories.

Another Stratemeyer Syndicate girl detective series published during the same time period is Billie Bradley. Scholar Deidre Johnson argues that the Stratemeyer pattern changes in this series, since Billie is "neither an orphan nor facing hostile surroundings."[34] Unlike Ruth Fielding, who worked for her money, Billie comes into a fortune when her aunt bequeaths her a house and valuable collections of coins and stamps. Billie can now afford boarding school at Three Towers Hall, where she meets friends Violet Farrington and Laura Jordon. Popular Billie leads a school rebellion when two nasty teachers are left to care for the students in *Billie Bradley at Three Towers Hall*. Like Ruth Fielding and Betty Gordon before her, Billie Bradley solves mysteries everywhere she goes.

With the Billie Bradley series, Edward Stratemeyer began fine-tuning his single-character girls' series, presenting readers with a spunky, well-to-do girl detective who could focus on other people's problems, because her own physical, emotional, and financial well-being was already established. Stratemeyer learned from Ruth Fielding that his protagonists should remain the same age throughout the series and that they should be somewhat distanced from the real world, and thus, his series would probably have a longer shelf life. With these thoughts in mind, Stratemeyer created another independent, wealthy, teenaged girl sleuth in 1929. "She might be called Nell Cody, Stratemeyer thought. Or Stella Strong. Or Nan Nelson, Diana Dare, or Helen Hale. Or, possibly, Nan Drew," biographer Melanie Rehak reports.[35] But no one, not even Stratemeyer himself, knew that his next girls' series would be the most popular and enduring girls' series ever published.

Notes

1. Lucy Rollin, *Twentieth-Century Teen Culture by the Decades* (Westport, CT: Greenwood, 1999), 3.

2. Nancy Tillman Romalov, "Mobile Heroines: Early Twentieth-Century Girls' Automobile Series," *Journal of Popular Culture*, 28.4 (1995), http://proquest.umi.com (accessed January 23, 2007).

3. Laura Dent Crane, *The Automobile Girls at Washington* (Philadelphia, PA: Henry Altemus, 1913), www.gutenberg.org (accessed January 23, 2007).

4. Crane, *The Automobile Girls at Washington.*

5. Crane, *The Automobile Girls at Washington.*

6. Laura Lee Hope, *The Outdoor Girls of Deepdale* (New York: Grosset & Dunlap, 1913), 99.

7. Hope, *The Outdoor Girls of Deepdale*, 116–17.

8. Romalov, "Mobile Heroines."

9. Hope, *The Outdoor Girls of Deepdale*, 68.

10. Bobbie Ann Mason, *The Girl Sleuth* (Athens: University of Georgia Press, 1995), 12.

11. Rollin, *Twentieth-Century Teen Culture by the Decades*, 28.

12. Vera Charlotte Scott Cushman, *Encyclopædia Britannica Online*, http://search.eb.com/eb/article-9125448 (accessed April 13, 2007).

13. Melanie Rehak, *Girl Sleuth: Nancy Drew and the Women Who Created Her* (Orlando, FL: Harcourt, Inc., 2005), 98.

14. Ilana Nash, *American Sweethearts: Teenage Girls in Twentieth-Century Popular Culture* (Bloomington: Indiana University Press, 2006), 32.

15. Ellen Singleton, "Camps and Tramps: Civilization, Culture, and the Use of Leisure in Early Twentieth-Century Outdoor Adventure Series Books for Girls and Boys," *Leisure/Loisir*, 29.1 (2005): 66.

16. Margaret Vandercook, *The Camp Fire Girls at Sunrise Hill* (Philadelphia, PA: J. C. Winston, 1913), www.gutenberg.org (accessed May 1, 2007).

17. Singleton, "Camps and Tramps," 67.

18. Romalov, "Mobile Heroines."

19. Carol Billman, *The Secret of the Stratemeyer Syndicate* (New York: Ungar, 1986), 57.

20. Billman, *The Secret of the Stratemeyer Syndicate*, 59.

21. Alice B. Emerson, *Ruth Fielding in Moving Pictures* (New York: Cupples & Leon, 1916), www.gutenberg.org (accessed October 11, 2005).

22. Alice B. Emerson, *Ruth Fielding in the Red Cross* (New York: Cupples & Leon, 1918), 50.

23. Billman, *The Secret of the Stratemeyer Syndicate*, 67.

24. Rollin, *Twentieth-Century Teen Culture by the Decades*, 19.

25. Billman, *The Secret of the Stratemeyer Syndicate*, 66.

26. Deidre Johnson, *Edward Stratemeyer and the Stratemeyer Syndicate* (New York: Twayne, 1993), 110.

27. Rehak, *Girl Sleuth*, 105.

28. Billman, *The Secret of the Stratemeyer Syndicate*, 67.

29. Billman, *The Secret of the Stratemeyer Syndicate*, 75.

30. Alice B. Emerson, *Ruth Fielding and Her Crowning Victory* (New York: Cupples & Leon, 1934), 210.

31. Johnson, *Edward Stratemeyer and the Stratemeyer Syndicate*, 114.

32. Alice B. Emerson, *Betty Gordon in Washington* (New York: Cupples & Leon, 1920), www.gutenberg.org (accessed January 23, 2007).

33. Society of Phantom Friends, *The Girls' Series Companion* (Rheem Valley, CA: SynSine, 1997), 53.

34. Johnson, *Edward Stratemeyer and the Stratemeyer Syndicate*, 115.

35. Rehak, *Girl Sleuth*, 109.

4

𝒢

The Secret of Nancy Drew and Her Sister Sleuths

The Nancy Drew Mystery Stories launched on April 28, 1930, marking the most important event in twentieth-century juvenile series book publishing. Series creator Edward Stratemeyer lived just long enough to see the first books in the series published. After their father's death, Stratemeyer's daughters, Harriet Adams and Edna Stratemeyer, tried to sell the Stratemeyer Syndicate, but no one wanted to buy a children's book publishing business during the Depression, so the sisters decided to run the company themselves. Adams and Stratemeyer spent the 1930s developing Nancy Drew into the perfect girl sleuth based on their own upper-class upbringing and then created new series featuring Nancy Drew clones that fit into a standard story formula. Ghostwriter Mildred Wirt worked for the Stratemeyer Syndicate throughout much of the decade, writing books in the Nancy Drew, Ruth Fielding, Doris Force, Kay Tracey, and The Dana Girls series. Wirt, a professional journalist, wrote series books to earn extra money, and by the end of the decade she had created her own girls' series, including Penny Nichols and Penny Parker.

The mystery genre dominated the girls' series book market in the 1930s, and Nancy Drew and her Stratemeyer Syndicate sisters found close cousins in Margaret Sutton's Judy Bolton Mystery Series and Clair

Blank's The Beverly Gray College Mystery Series. It is important to note that teen girls were often depicted in girls' series books as being wealthier than many readers would have been during the Great Depression. Girls' mystery series offered readers the fantasies of financial well-being and the freedom of independence that many teen girls simply didn't have during the 1930s. These fantasies were exactly what readers wanted—a way to escape the economic realities of everyday life. Moreover, crime and justice were popular themes in American society during the 1930s, fueled by the kidnapping of the Lindbergh baby and the unlawful activities of such young criminals as Bonnie and Clyde. Girls' mystery series reduced criminals to stupid, evil people who could be captured by such smart, brave teens as Nancy Drew and Judy Bolton.

Nancy Drew and Her Sister Sleuths: Stratemeyer Syndicate Girls' Mystery Series

In 1929, Edward Stratemeyer decided to create more girls' series focusing on a single heroine, similar to the Ruth Fielding series. Stratemeyer wanted to hire Ruth Fielding ghostwriter Mildred Wirt for this new series. Stratemeyer sent Grosset & Dunlap a proposal for the Stella Strong Stories, which were mysteries featuring a teenage girl sleuth. He proposed five stories to begin the series, including *Stella Strong at Mystery Towers*, *The Mystery at Shadow Ranch*, *The Disappearance of Nellie Ray*, *The Missing Box of Diamonds*, and *The Secret of the Old Clock*. The proposed stories were similar to the Stratemeyer Syndicate's popular The Hardy Boys series and featured mysteries involving crooks, missing treasures, and long-lost heirs.

Stratemeyer quickly hired Mildred Wirt to write three books for the series, titled *The Secret of the Old Clock*, *The Hidden Staircase*, and *The Bungalow Mystery*, which were to be published by Grosset & Dunlap under the pseudonym Carolyn Keene. She was paid $125 per manuscript.[1] Wirt got to work on *The Secret of the Old Clock*, following Stratemeyer's instructions that the stories be "brave and adventurous."[2] Sixteen days after Stratemeyer sent Wirt his instructions for the Nancy Drew Mystery Stories, the stock market crashed, ushering in the Great Depression. On October 29, 1929, often referred to as Black Tuesday, "stock values plummeted by $14 billion," destroying the U.S. economy and leaving many people unemployed.[3] Nevertheless, Stratemeyer's business continued, and Wirt wrote *The Secret of the Old Clock*, a story featuring the selfish and wealthy Topham family, whose money ironically came from the stock market; two virtuous, poor girls; a sick, elderly woman; and a missing will that would benefit the needy women and deny the mean, undeserving Tophams. While Wirt biographer Melanie Rehak suggests that Edward Stratemeyer actually wrote the opening lines of *The Secret of the Old Clock*, Wirt describes her efforts to begin the story:

> I typed a sentence or two, and threw them away. Then full-blown, a paragraph flashed into my mind: "It would be a shame if all that money went to the Tophams! They will fly higher than ever." Self-assured, ready at the drop of a typewriter key to help the downtrodden by righting a wrong, Nancy herself had spoken.[4]

Sixteen-year-old Nancy Drew has already graduated from high school, and she is responsible for managing the family household, with the help of housekeeper Hannah Gruen. Since her mother died when she was three, Nancy is very close to her father, Carson Drew, who often consults her on his legal cases. Although she had been popular at school, Nancy's only friend early in the series is Helen Corning. In the fictional mid-western town of River Heights, Nancy enjoys sports, clubs, and parties, living the life of a "well-to-do plucky girl of the twenties."[5] Her blonde curly hair in a stylish bob, Nancy wears fashionable clothes, including tweed suits, cloche hats, and fancy dresses. She drives a shiny blue roadster, a birthday present from her father. Wirt describes the world inhabited by Nancy Drew in the early 1930s:

> Dramatic changes soon came to the world, especially in communication, transportation, and the attitude of people. Through it all, Nancy, as I envisioned her, stood rock-firm, untouched by war, the Depression, economic or moral problems—a trustworthy symbol for parents and children.[6]

Nancy is initially described in the first book as a typical 1930s "sub-deb," a high society teenage girl not quite old enough for her official debut in society. Teen culture historian Ilana Nash explains that during the Depression, not many girls fit the sub-deb mold, even though the sub-deb was the most common portrayal of teen girls in popular culture. Instead, many teens looked for work, and if they couldn't find it, they either went to school or joined other teen hobos traveling the country by train, searching for work. Most teen girls stayed home and sold newspapers, babysat, or worked in textile mills to earn money for their families.[7] Nevertheless, "[t]he sub-deb dominated representations of girls, even though the vast majority of American girls did not conform to this mold—and many, significantly, lived in distressed circumstances at the opposite end of the spectrum."[8]

As *The Secret of the Old Clock* progresses, however, Nancy is portrayed as much more than the "gracious, well-to-do, and largely decorative" sub-deb.[9] She is brave, independent, intelligent, stubborn, and empathetic. In this first book, Nancy decides to find Josiah Crowley's missing will to help the poor Horner girls and elderly Abigail Rowen live a better life. In the second book in the series, *The Hidden Staircase*, Nancy helps twin spinsters Floretta and Rosemary Turnbull save their home from evil con man Nathan Gombet, who tries to scare the sisters into selling him their house. Gombet also kidnaps Carson Drew, and when Nancy solves the mystery, she inadvertently rescues her father. When Nancy realizes her father is a prisoner, she leaps into action: "Without a thought for her own safety, now that she knew her father was in danger, she flung open the door."[10] Carson Drew is so impressed with his daughter's detection skills that he decides to hire her: "From this day on I intend to turn over my mystery cases to you. . . . As a detective, you have me backed completely off the map."[11] Nancy likes being thought of as a real detective, and soon she is solving *The Bungalow Mystery*, saving a young woman from her evil guardian. Nancy gains a reputation as an amateur detective and everyone respects her.

Although Wirt later said Edward Stratemeyer found her characterization of Nancy Drew disappointing because she was too assertive, researchers have found no record of Stratemeyer's negative reactions to his new girl sleuth.[12] Scholars have argued that Nancy's success comes from "her personal and financial independence and her strong character."[13] Many years after writing *The Secret of the Old Clock*, Wirt wrote that Nancy suddenly "exploded into a vibrant ball of energy, unfettered, eternally seeking adventure and challenge."[14] Author Bobbie Ann Mason explains the appeal of Nancy Drew:

Not only is Nancy perfect, but she possesses the ideal qualities of each age and sex: child, girl, teenager, boy, and adult. She has made a daring stride into adulthood, and she also trespasses into male territory without giving up female advantages.[15]

Besides having a fabulous new heroine, Stratemeyer had plotted perfect stories to attract young readers during the early days of the Depression. The focus on missing wills, lost heirs, and stolen jewels were appealing to girls who had little money and few luxury items. Moreover, the stories contained familiar Gothic elements, including the motherless heroine; spooky old houses; ghosts, dark, stormy weather; and confined spaces, like the hidden staircase and the locked closet, where Nancy is often trapped. Unlike traditional Gothic romance, however, Nancy usually frees herself, rather than waiting for men to rescue her. Carol Billman, Stratemeyer Syndicate historian, argues that Nancy Drew is "Gothicized detection from which all prospect of growing up and sexual discovery has been removed and that psychological distress will never be known by the outgoing, no-nonsense girl detective."[16]

Stratemeyer knew Nancy Drew was going to be popular. "The combination of Stratemeyer's outline and editing with Mildred's efforts had produced a fantasy girl. . . . Together they had created a star, and Stratemeyer knew it," Rehak contends.[17] Sales of the early books were strong, and the Syndicate had another successful girls' series. But Stratemeyer didn't live to see the popularity of his new heroine. He died of pneumonia on May 10, 1930, twelve days after the first books in the Nancy Drew Mystery Stories were launched. When his daughters realized that there were no buyers for the business, they decided to learn everything they could about their father's business and continue to publish series fiction for children and teens. Since Stratemeyer hadn't taught them much about his business, this was a big job.

Adams had worked as a junior editor for her father after her graduation from Wellesley College and before her marriage fifteen years earlier, but Stratemeyer had expected her to work at home, behind the scenes. As Adams told one reporter, "His standards were strict, and he didn't believe women should work. If they did it was a disgrace, and it meant their fathers couldn't support them."[18] Adams relished the idea of running the Stratemeyer Syndicate. Rehak reports, "For Harriet . . . it was the chance of a lifetime. . . . Not only would she be able to work, as she had so wanted to do after college, but she would be the boss."[19]

Harriet Otis Smith, Stratemeyer's secretary, worked with Adams and Stratemeyer to save the Stratemeyer Syndicate. Stratemeyer worked on the bookkeeping at home, and Adams became the public face of the business, dealing with publishers and learning the structure of the business. Meanwhile, Smith worked to complete manuscripts already drafted, including the fourth Nancy Drew story, *The Mystery at Lilac Inn*. Wirt reported that she was asked to make changes in the series: "*Lilac Inn* marked minor changes in writing style and in Nancy's character. The syndicate's new owner asked that I make the sleuth less bold."[20]

Before leaving the Stratemeyer Syndicate at the close of 1930, Smith created cousins Bess Marvin and George Fayne, who became Nancy's crime-solving companions. In 1931, Wirt wrote *The Secret at Shadow Ranch*, where she introduced athletic tomboy George and plump, feminine Bess. Rehak argues that readers found Nancy's new friends appealing because "if you were not as perfect as Nancy, you were at least interesting enough to be like—and thus to be—one of the closest chums of the queen bee."[21]

In *The Secret at Shadow Ranch*, Nancy joins Bess and George on a visit to their uncle's Arizona ranch, where Nancy helps a young woman find her father. Adams continued to change Nancy's character in this story, making her meeker. Wirt wrote two more books in the series, *The Secret at Red Gate Farm* and *The Clue in the Diary* in 1932. *The Clue in the Diary* is noteworthy because it introduces Nancy's boyfriend, Ned Nickerson, whom editors Adams and Stratemeyer created as "filler."[22] When the sisters tried to hire Wirt to do more books in the series for a reduced salary of $100 per manuscript at the height of the Depression, they were surprised when she turned them down.[23] Not only was Wirt writing the Nancy Drew Mystery Stories, she also wrote their Ruth Fielding and Doris Force books. But Wirt had been hired to write several books for other publishers, and she didn't want to work for a reduced salary. So Adams hired Walter Karig, who was already a practiced Stratemeyer Syndicate ghostwriter, to write both Nancy Drew and Doris Force. Karig wrote *Nancy's Mysterious Letter*, *The Sign of the Twisted Candles*, and *The Password to Larkspur Lane* for the Nancy Drew series.

Several years later, Adams learned that Karig had violated his contract with the Stratemeyer Syndicate when he wrote the Library of Congress requesting credit for the books he had authored. The Library of Congress mistakenly assumed he had written all the books in the various Stratemeyer Syndicate series. Adams convinced the Library of Congress to maintain the secrecy of the Stratemeyer Syndicate's ghostwriters, and the pseudonymous Carolyn Keene remained on record as the author of the Nancy Drew Mystery Stories.

By 1932, the Stratemeyer Syndicate was feeling the economic crunch of the Depression. As Rehak reports, "Sales of many Syndicate series slowed down, and publishers canceled orders—Doris Force . . . did not last past 1932, and the Outdoor Girls, the Blythe Girls . . . among others, were gone by 1933."[24] Wirt returned to write the final books in the Ruth Fielding series, which had faltered in popularity after career girl Ruth became a wife and mother. With several of their popular girls' series gone, Adams and Stratemeyer decided to create the Kay Tracey and The Dana Girls series to fill the void, and they hired Wirt to write them. Both Kay Tracey and The Dana Girls series used the same Gothic elements found in Nancy Drew.

The Kay Tracey series features a sixteen-year-old blonde, brown-eyed teen who lives with her mother and older cousin Bill. Kay's best friends are twins Betty and Wilma Worth. Blonde Betty is fun and sparkly, while brunette Wilma is dreamy and poetic. Kay is the natural leader of the group. The girls attend Carmont High School, along with a nasty girl named Ethel Eaton and Kay's favorite date, Ronnie Earle. In *The Secret of the Red Scarf*, published in 1934, Kay and her friends help Dick Ludlow, whom they find injured after he is thrown from his horse. When they learn Dick is searching for his missing sister, Kay locates Helene Ludlow, and she reunites the siblings.

While the series had much in common with Nancy Drew, Kay Tracey was a pale imitation. Like Nancy, Kay frequently encounters danger, and she is often kidnapped, tied up, or knocked out by thieves. But somehow, the stories just weren't as appealing as the Nancy Drew series. *The Girls' Series Companion* states, "Kay Tracey books are a bit like comic books; lurid, but too cartoonish to be frightening."[25] Nevertheless, the series was popular enough to produce new stories for the next eight years, until World War II, when a paper shortage likely resulted in its cancellation.[26] Readers, however, had not seen the last of Kay Tracey. The series reappeared numerous times over the next five decades.

If Kay Tracey was a Nancy Drew imposter, The Dana Girls were a female version of the Stratemeyer Syndicate's popular series The Hardy Boys. To ensure the series' success, Adams hired Leslie McFarlane, the Canadian ghostwriter of The Hardy Boys, to write the first four books. McFarlane recalls, "It was 1934 and things were tough. I felt almighty foolish about becoming Carolyn Keene, but my wife promised she wouldn't tell anyone. . . . Then the whole thing became too much for me and I begged off. Starvation seemed preferable."[27] In this new series, teen orphans Jean and Louise Dana have guardians in Uncle Ned and Aunt Harriet. Uncle Ned, a ship's captain, is often away at sea. In his absence, Aunt Harriet and the headmistress of Starhurst boarding school give the girls freedom to solve mysteries.

The Dana Girls encounter their first mystery in *By the Light of the Study Lamp*. In this story, published in 1934, Uncle Ned notes women's changing roles in society:

> "I daresay we could solve the mystery of this lamp quite as well as any man could," declared Jean. "I think we'd make good detectives if we had a chance."
>
> "There's the modern girl for you, Mr. Starr," [Uncle Ned] said. "Think they can do anything. It's not a man's world anymore."[28]

Instead of being a commentary on women's equality, however, it is more likely that Adams and Stratemeyer were commenting on their own situation as successful businesswomen, rather than any real gains made by women in the workplace. In the early 1930s, women who were full-time homemakers found clerical and social service jobs out of necessity. During the Depression, women were often able to find low-paying employment more readily than men. "Many fathers and husbands resented wives and daughters who had taken over their breadwinning roles," report John M. Murrin and colleagues.[29] Moreover, President Roosevelt's "New Deal offered . . . female reformers little opportunity to advance the cause of women's equality."[30] Instead, the women's movement of the 1930s focused on protective legislation to safeguard female workers, who were considered more fragile than men.

Much as Adams and Stratemeyer got the opportunity to run their father's business, Jean and Louise Dana accidentally get the chance to become detectives, and they help their friend, Evelyn Starr, locate her missing brother and the Starr family jewels. They also thwart the evil Jake Garbone and his sister Faye Violette, who want to steal the Starr family fortune, and Lettie Briggs, their enemy at school. Similar stories followed for seven more titles in the series during the 1930s, with Mildred Wirt taking over as series writer for Leslie McFarlane in 1936. The Dana Girls mysteries featured thieves, con artists, long-lost heirs, and orphans.

By the end of the decade, Adams was much more interested in the Stratemeyer Syndicate business than her sister. In the late 1930s, Stratemeyer got married and had a baby, leaving the Stratemeyer Syndicate work to Adams. Despite the introduction of new girls' series, Nancy Drew continued to be the Stratemeyer Syndicate's most important asset, and Adams sought ways to capitalize on her famous teen queen. Since movies featuring teens were popular during the second half of the decade, like the Andy Hardy films starring Mickey Rooney, it is no surprise that Hollywood came knocking on Adams's door. In the late 1930s, she sold the rights to the Nancy Drew stories for $6,000 for a series of films produced by Warner Bros.[31] Warner Bros. produced four movies starring Bonita Granville as Nancy Drew, including *Nancy Drew Detective*, *Nancy Drew Reporter*, *Nancy Drew Trouble Shooter*, and *Nancy Drew and the Hidden Staircase*. Nash argues,

> Very little of Carolyn's Keene's Nancy remains in the films. Instead, the Nancy offered by Warner Bros. is markedly younger, more inept, and generally less admirable than her literary counterpart. Filmic Nancy pointedly lacks the personhood inherent in literary Nancy, creating an astonishingly abrupt alteration of the character's meaning.[32]

Bonita Granville's portrayal of Nancy Drew was overtly sexual, and a sexual relationship between Nancy and her father is inferred in the movies. In a shocking scene in *Nancy Drew Reporter*, Carson Drew carries teenage Nancy to her bed, singing the song "Pretty Baby." Carson is portrayed as Nancy's protector, and possibly, her lover. This scene shows how the ideal teenage girl is admired both for her woman's body, and conversely, her childish behavior. Moreover, ads for the Nancy Drew movies suggest she is stupid, making fun of her poor spelling and bad grades. Warner Bros. pressed the traditional sub-deb definition onto Nancy, "leasing the name and likeness of Bonita Granville to the Lane Company, a manufacturer of hope chests."[33] Strangely, both Adams and Mildred Wirt appeared to like the Nancy Drew movies, despite the "evisceration" of their literary heroine.[34] By the end of 1940, the Nancy Drew Mystery Stories had sold approximately two and a half million copies.[35]

Nancy Drew's Cousins:
Judy Bolton, Beverly Gray, and Penny Parker

After her marriage in 1924, Rachel Beebe Sutton began writing stories for her stepdaughter, Dorothy. "By 1930, Dorothy was reading the Ruth Fielding series and [Sutton] decided to turn her 'Melissa of Dry Brook Hollow' stories, which were based on experiences from childhood, into published books," reports series book collector John Axe.[36] A literary agent found a publisher for Sutton's books with Grosset & Dunlap, who changed the protagonist's name to Judy Bolton. The publisher also decided Sutton's pen name would be Margaret. Sutton later changed her first name to Margaret, making her the only girls' series author on record to legally assume her pen name. Reflecting on the beginnings of her writing career in an interview at the University of Wisconsin in 1984, Sutton stated, "[I]f I'd known about the Stratemeyer Syndicate I probably never would have attempted to write a series of books."[37]

But in 1932, Sutton didn't know about the Stratemeyer Syndicate, so she published her first Judy Bolton Mystery, *The Vanishing Shadow*, with Grosset & Dunlap. Fifteen-year-old Judy Bolton and her family live in fictional Roulsville, which is based on Sutton's hometown of Austin, Pennsylvania. When Judy discovers that the Roulsville Dam is poorly constructed, she informs her brother, Horace. He becomes a hero when he warns the town the dam is about to burst, saving everyone from a flood that destroys Roulsville. Like many details in Sutton's books, this event was based on the very real Austin Flood of 1911, which Sutton survived as a child. Although it is Judy who discovers the danger in the story, Horace becomes the hero, rather than Judy. Judy has a chance to tell how she learned about the shabbily constructed dam, however, when the construction workers are tried in court.

Red-haired Judy is portrayed as a typical teenage girl who spends a lot of time with friends and family. Judy is expected to help her mother with the housework, although as Bobbie Ann Mason points out, Judy's housekeeping skills are limited: "Judy is an individualist who doesn't give a hoot about housecleaning, can't sew, and can just barely make a gooseberry pie."[38] Instead, Judy craves adventure. In *The Vanishing Shadow*, she notes that boys experience more adventure than girls, and she laments, "Sometimes I wish I were a boy."[39] Nevertheless, Judy finds mysteries to solve, and she gains a reputation as an amateur detective amongst her family and friends. Middle-class Judy may not have a car to help her get around, but she manages to solve mysteries anyway, often with the help of family and friends.

Like the Stratemeyer Syndicate mysteries, Gothic elements are in abundance, including shadows, ghosts, phantoms, and haunted houses. For instance, in *The Haunted Attic*, Judy investigates a ghost in the Bolton's new house. The Judy Bolton series differs in a number of ways, however, from the contemporary Stratemeyer Syndicate girls' series. Judy is still in high school when the series opens, so she can't take up sleuthing full time like Nancy Drew. Unlike Stratemeyer Syndicate sleuths, Judy comes from a middle-class family, and the books display more concern for ordinary people trying to survive during the Depression than Stratemeyer Syndicate books. Judy also ages as the series progresses, a practice the Stratemeyer Syndicate gave up after their Ruth Fielding series waned in popularity as Ruth became a career woman, wife, and mother. As Judy grows up, she becomes interested in romance and marriage, and her suitors seem more human than the Stratemeyer Syndicate "filler" boyfriends.

After she graduates from high school in 1936 in *The Mysterious Half-Cat*, Judy is torn between Peter Dobbs and Arthur Farringdon-Pett. By 1937, she secretly agrees to marry Arthur in *The Riddle of the Double Ring*, but she breaks off the engagement. She later decides to marry Peter, who shares her interest in solving mysteries, in *The Name on the Bracelet*. Even with a married heroine, the Judy Bolton series carried on for three more decades. While Judy accepts a traditional role that Nancy Drew rejects, she also subverts the patriarchal structure of society by becoming an amateur detective.

Some critics argue that the writing of a single author who based the series on her real life experiences, along with strong characterization, were the secrets to the success of the Judy Bolton series. Judy seems more real to readers, more like themselves, than the Stratemeyer Syndicate fantasy heroines. Perhaps this explains why the series is the "longest running and most popular girls' series ever written by a single author rather than a syndicate."[40]

In 1934, publisher A. L. Burt introduced another new girls' series, The Beverly Gray College Mystery Series, written by teen author Clair Blank. In *Beverly Gray Freshman*, Beverly is introduced as a young college student who wants a career and wants to make friends on her own, rather than trade on her mother's reputation at Vernon College. Before long, beautiful Beverly builds her own positive reputation at the college, making many friends and suitors. She becomes friends with actress Shirley Parker, artist Lois Mason, and fun Lenora Whitehill. Beverly has two suitors, hometown boyfriend Jim Stanton and aviator Larry Owens.

Stories in the Beverly Gray series feature several plots, and Beverly often solves more than one mystery. In the first book, Beverly deals with Halloween pranks, locates her missing short story, keeps her lonely roommate from running away, saves her roommate during a fire, and stops Shirley's jealous boyfriend from attacking them and extorting money from Shirley. Bev is also captured by a woman hermit after she gets lost in a snowstorm during the Christmas holiday. From the very first book, Beverly Gray was known for her exciting adventures:

> She is kidnapped 26 times, attacked by wild animals seven times, trapped in three violent storms and three earthquakes, shot at twice, menaced by Gypsies, captured by cannibals on two separate occasions, washed overboard, and nearly trapped in a raging fire; still she emerges with every hair in place, to the relief of her friends and the astonishment of her readers.[41]

By 1935, Beverly is a college graduate ready to start her career. In *Beverly Gray's Career*, Beverly's parents agree to let her move with friends to New York to pursue work in newspapers and publishing. Beverly turns down her father's offer of an allowance: "I'm—I want to do everything myself. I don't want money coming in just as though I didn't need a job. I'm going to make my own living myself! Don't you see? I want to depend on myself—not somebody else."[42] Beverly is portrayed as an ambitious, independent career woman. After three weeks of hunting, Beverly gets a job at the *New York Herald Tribune* newspaper. She also has many other adventures, including helping hungry children, solving a murder mystery, and catching jewel thieves. During the last half of the 1930s, she travels abroad to Europe, India, and Asia, reporting on world events and chasing evil villains. Although Blank never traveled to the exotic locations visited by Beverly, she researched her settings carefully. Despite the research, critics suggest that Blank's writing was not very good, and the popularity of the series can be attributed to her adventurous and independent protagonist.

Even while she was writing for the Stratemeyer Syndicate series, Wirt also had her own girls' series during the 1930s, including Penny Nichols (under the pseudonym Joan Clark) and Penny Parker. Over time, Adams and Stratemeyer were writing longer outlines for Stratemeyer Syndicate books, leaving less room for creativity on Wirt's part, and Wirt wanted to write her own girls' series. When Penny Nichols failed to catch on, Wirt started again with the Penny Parker series in 1939. Sixteen-year-old Penny has blue eyes and curly blonde hair and is a champion swimmer and diver. "Penny would soon become Mildred's favorite of her characters, perhaps because she bore more than a little resemblance to her creator," suggests biographer Rehak.[43] Years later, Wirt fondly remembered Penny Parker: "The Penny Parker Mystery Stories . . . especially appealed to me because without editorial direction, I was able to create a Nancy-type character, a bit flip perhaps, but entirely to my liking."[44]

Like Beverly Gray and her author, Wirt, high school sophomore Penny wants to become a reporter, but her efforts to help her publisher father at the *Riverview Star* often find her entangled in mystery. Like Bess Marvin in the Nancy Drew series, Penny's best friend, Louise Siddell, is an unwilling detection companion, but Penny doesn't let Louise keep her from solving mysteries. In *Tale of the Witch Doll*, Penny helps actress Helene Harmon solve the mystery of the reappearing witch doll, which Helene believes is responsible for her accidents and bad luck. Penny writes a front-page story for her father's newspaper about the capture of the evil man who sought revenge on Helene and her brother. In *The Vanishing Houseboat*, Penny solves two mysteries, learning why people are disappearing from a boarding house and find-ing a stolen houseboat.

The Penny Parker series ran for eight years, ceasing publication in 1947. Critics suggest there were two problems with the series that en-sured its downfall in the late 1940s. First, Wirt used many ethnic stereotypes and undereducated rural people in her stories, making "Penny (and Wirt) seem rather prejudiced and intolerant."[45] Second, Wirt took the opportunity to set her own series firmly in the present, unlike the books she wrote for the Stratemeyer Syndicate, dating the series to World War II. Despite her experience writing girls' series for the Stratemeyer Syndicate, it is noteworthy that Wirt's Penny Parker series was probably not very popular with readers. Perhaps this is be-cause she strayed from the Stratemeyer Syndicate's winning formulas. Although her own series ceased publication, Wirt continued to write for the Stratemeyer Syndicate until 1953.

Nurse Helen Dore Boylston, who worked with the British Expedi-tionary Force during World War I and the European Red Cross, began publishing her series about teen nursing student Sue Barton in 1936. Sue and her new friends, Kit and Connie, find the hospital exciting, with needy patients, scary laundry men, amorous doctors, and catty nurses. Sue solves the occasional mystery during her training, but the emphasis is on nursing in these stories. By the end of her studies, Sue is ready for her nursing career, and she wants to work before marrying Dr. Bill Barry. Julia Hallam reports, "The nursing profession took a dim view of women who married; marriage effectively terminated their careers."[46] Indeed, Sue's friend Connie gives up nursing when she gets married, while the unmarried Sue and Kit continue working. Sue is often torn between her career and her marriage plans. Sue pleads with Bill:

> But—could I—please not get married just yet? I've hardly—begun—to do things. I've wanted so much to be a nurse, and I've worked so hard. I know, as your wife, I can still be a nurse if I want to—but *not on my own!*[47]

Sue asks Bill to keep their engagement secret and he agrees. Sue and her friend Kit move to New York City to work with the Henry Street Nurses, founded by public health advocate Lillian Wald, in *Sue Barton,*

Visiting Nurse. When Sue tells Bill she wants to spend two years work-ing in New York City, he accuses her of being a career girl who keeps "men dangling half their lives."[48] Sue and Bill break up for a few months, but by the end of the story, the engagement is back on. The death of Bill's father postpones their wedding in *Sue Barton, Rural Nurse,* so Sue works as a public health nurse in New Hampshire, help-ing Bill find the source of a typhoid epidemic and caring for patients during a hurricane.

Sue and Bill finally marry in *Sue Barton, Superintendent of Nurses.* While Sue enjoys her job as the head of a small nursing school, at the end of the book she informs Bill she is resigning because she is preg-nant. Published in 1940, *Superintendent of Nurses* was supposed to be the last book in the Sue Barton series. Boylston continued writing for teens with the Carol Page series, the story of a young actress based on the life of her friend, Eva La Gallienne, in the early 1940s. But girls' se-ries featuring teen nurses were very popular during World War II, and beloved Nurse Sue Barton Barry, whose books "sold millions of copies in the United States and England," made a postwar comeback.[49]

While mystery series featuring amateur girl sleuths dominated the market in the 1930s, Sue Barton, Beverly Gray, and Penny Parker sig-naled the beginning of another trend at the end of the decade. By the early 1940s, popular girls' series books featured teen protagonists who combine amateur sleuthing with careers, working in traditional female roles as nurses, flight attendants, and actresses.

Notes

1. Melanie Rehak, *Girl Sleuth: Nancy Drew and the Women Who Created Her* (Orlando, FL: Harcourt, 2005), 114.

2. Rehak, *Girl Sleuth,* 114.

3. John M. Murrin, Paul E. Johnson, James M. McPherson, Alice Fahs, and Gary Gerstle, *Liberty, Equality, and Power: A History of the American People* (Belmont, CA: Thomson Wadsworth, 2006), 893.

4. Mildred Wirt Benson, "The Nancy I Knew," introduction to *The Mystery at Lilac Inn,* by Carolyn Keene (1931; reprint, Bedford, MA: Applewood Books, 1994), ii–iii.

5. Rehak, *Girl Sleuth,* 116.

6. Benson, "The Nancy I Knew," iii.

7. Lucy Rollin, *Twentieth-Century Teen Culture by the Decades* (Westport, CT: Greenwood, 1999), 82.

8. Ilana Nash, *American Sweethearts: Teenage Girls in Twentieth-Century Popular Culture* (Bloomington: Indiana University Press, 2006), 102.

9. Nash, *American Sweethearts*, 98.

10. Carolyn Keene, *The Hidden Staircase* (1930; reprint, Bedford, MA: Applewood Books, 1992), 193.

11. Keene, *The Hidden Staircase*, 206.

12. Nash, *American Sweethearts*, 33.

13. Deidre Johnson, *Edward Stratemeyer and the Stratemeyer Syndicate* (New York: Twayne, 1993), 151.

14. Benson, "The Nancy I Knew," i.

15. Bobbie Ann Mason, *The Girl Sleuth* (Athens: University of Georgia Press, 1995), 53.

16. Carol Billman, *The Secret of the Stratemeyer Syndicate* (New York: Ungar, 1986), 118.

17. Rehak, *Girl Sleuth*, 119.

18. Maria Lenhart, "Whodunit, Nancy Drew?" *Christian Science Monitor* (May 11, 1979): 12.

19. Rehak, *Girl Sleuth*, 135.

20. Benson, "The Nancy I Knew," vii.

21. Rehak, *Girl Sleuth*, 142.

22. Rehak, *Girl Sleuth*, 169.

23. Rehak, *Girl Sleuth*, 149–50.

24. Rehak, *Girl Sleuth*, 161.

25. Society of Phantom Friends, *The Girls' Series Companion* (Rheem Valley, CA: SynSine, 1997), 264.

26. John Axe, *The Secret of Collecting Girls' Series Books* (Grantsville, MD: Hobby House, 2000), 105.

27. Leslie McFarlane, *Ghost of the Hardy Boys* (New York: Two Continents, 1976), 198–99.

28. Carolyn Keene, *By the Light of the Study Lamp* (New York: Grosset & Dunlap, 1934), 49.

29. Murrin et al., *Liberty, Equality, and Power*, 923.

30. Murrin et al., *Liberty, Equality, and Power*, 923.

31. Rehak, *Girl Sleuth*, 191.

32. Nash, *American Sweethearts*, 72.

33. Nash, *American Sweethearts*, 106.

34. Nash, *American Sweethearts*, 116.

35. Rehak, *Girl Sleuth*, 196.

36. Axe, *The Secret of Collecting Girls' Series Books*, 68.

37. *"Q and A with Margaret Sutton: From an Interview at the University of Wisconsin, June 23, 1984,"* www.judybolton.com/jbwisc.html (accessed March 29, 2007).

38. Mason, *The Girl Sleuth*, 84.

39. Margaret Sutton, *The Vanishing Shadow* (New York: Grosset & Dunlap, 1932), 53.

40. Society of Phantom Friends, *The Girls' Series Companion*, 241.

41. Society of Phantom Friends, *The Girls' Series Companion*, 57.

42. Clair Blank, *Beverly Gray's Career* (New York: Grosset & Dunlap, 1935), 21.

43. Rehak, *Girl Sleuth*, 201.

44. Mildred Wirt Benson, "More About Nancy," introduction to *The Secret at Shadow Ranch*, by Carolyn Keene (1931; reprint, Bedford, MA: Applewood Books, 1994), vii.

45. Axe, *The Secret of Collecting Girls' Series Books*, 121.

46. Julia Hallam, "Nursing an Image: The Sue Barton Career Novels," in *Image and Power: Women in Fiction in the Twentieth Century*, ed. Sarah Sceats and Gail Cunningham (London: Longman, 1996), 101.

47. Helen Dore Boylston, *Sue Barton, Senior Nurse* (Boston: Little, Brown and Company, 1937), 215–16.

48. Helen Dore Boylston, *Sue Barton, Visiting Nurse* (Boston: Little, Brown and Company, 1938), 197.

49. "Helen Dore Boylston," *Contemporary Authors Online* (Detroit: Gale, 2003), http://galenet.galgroup.com/servlet/LitRC (accessed October 2, 2007).

5

Career Girls and World War II

Mysteries, career stories, and romantic family series were popular with teen readers during the 1940s. World War II, which involved the United States from 1941 until 1945, had more impact on serial fiction written for girls than World War I. As John M. Murrin and colleagues explain, "A massive propaganda effort to bolster popular support for wartime sacrifice presented the conflict as a struggle to protect and preserve the American way of life."[1] Such products of popular culture as movies and books became part of this propaganda. Girls' series books published in the early 1940s portrayed young women who stayed on the home front supporting their boys, army nurses who cared for injured soldiers, and journalists who investigated spies. During the era of "Rosie the Riveter" and the early years of Wonder Woman, young women in girls' series books had the freedom to do just about anything writers could imagine.

Series like Janet Lambert's Parrish Family and Jordan Family featured proud and patriotic military families. "American teens shared in the wartime patriotism and seriousness, and then in the postwar euphoria and economic boom, just as they shared family and community life with adults," reports teen culture expert Lucy Rollin.[2] Penny Parrish is the ultimate 1940s teen bobbysoxer, leading the "practically perfect" life of a typical innocent teenage girl. Vivacious Penny's life focuses on fun and romance, even during wartime.

As more workers were needed during World War II, teen girls in series books became career women. Cherry Ames followed Sue Barton into nursing, where she worked as an army nurse. Journalists Penny Parker and Beverly Gray continued their exciting careers, investigating enemy spies and factory sabotage on the home front. After the war, the concept of "teenager" took hold in American society: "After 1944 the culture of the teenager . . . moved rapidly into the public spotlight."[3] *Seventeen* magazine debuted in 1944, creating a place to advertise products directly to teen girls. A demographics survey commissioned by *Seventeen* showed that teenage girls had money to spend on makeup, clothing, and accessories, and the publication helped to create a whole new market for products that could be sold to girls like the fictional "Teena" through advertisements in the magazine.[4] In 1945, "A Teenage Bill of Rights" was published in the *New York Times Magazine*, demanding the right to fun, freedom, and romance. In postwar America, dating became a popular activity among teens. Girls expected to have several steady boyfriends before they settled down.

But the idea of being a career woman struck a chord with young readers during the war years, and since career stories were so popular, such publishers as Grosset & Dunlap and Cupples & Leon continued to introduce new career girls to readers after the war. Vicki Barr became a flight stewardess, while Connie Blair worked in advertising. Since such mystery series as Nancy Drew, Kay Tracey, Judy Bolton, and The Dana Girls were so popular with teen readers, career women Cherry Ames, Vicki Barr, and Connie Blair became sleuths during and after the war. Near the end of the decade, younger girl detectives like Trixie Belden and Ginny Gordon were introduced to readers.

Romantic Family Stories

In the early 1940s, such romantic family stories as Janet Lambert's Parrish Family and Jordan Family series were popular with teen readers. Published in 1941, Lambert's *Star Spangled Summer* introduces fourteen-year-old Penny Parrish, who returns home from a visit with relatives, bringing her new friend Carrol Houghton. Home for Penny and the rest of the Parrish clan is an American army post, since her father is a military officer. While the Parrishes aren't wealthy like the

Houghtons, they are a very happy, loving family. Carrol thrives with the Parrishes, and when Penny writes a letter to Mr. Houghton telling him that he neglects his daughter, he arrives with his love and luxurious lifestyle to share with Carrol and the Parrish family. The families become the best of friends.

Dreams of Glory reunites Penny and Carrol at West Point, where Major Parrish is stationed and Penny's brother David is a student. The Parrish family spends time with the Houghtons in New York City, where a chance encounter with a famous actress leads Penny to an acting career. Despite the fact that these stories are set largely on military bases, the first two books neglect to mention the events of World War II. In fact, these books were likely written before the United States joined the war in December 1941.

In *Glory Be!*, published in 1943, Penny's eighteenth birthday celebration is interrupted by the start of the war. Dust-jacket blurbs outline the story: "A war time tragedy brings changes to Carrol's and Penny's families, but one of them becomes a military bride." Carrol marries David Parrish, becoming a pregnant war bride and a proper member of the Parrish family. But readers know Carrol will be all right, even if David doesn't return from war, because she has inherited her father's vast wealth. Throughout the series, Carrol and David are generous with their money, symbolizing the economic growth that took place in the United States during and after World War II. The Parrish family often refers to Carrol's wealth and generosity, recognizing the power the money gives the young woman who inherited it, rather than the young man who married it. Carrol makes sure everyone in the Parrish family has houses, cars, and other luxuries most military families couldn't afford or find during wartime. Ironically, Carrol's sharing invokes socialist ideals at a time in history when anticommunism was gaining strength in the United States.

One story, *Up Goes the Curtain*, is firmly anchored in the United States during World War II. Penny makes a trip home to Fort Knox to see her family, where she becomes jealous of her boyfriend Terry's attentions to a young woman visiting the army base. Penny steals a letter from the woman, and when she guiltily confesses her bad behavior and presents the letter to her parents, Colonel Parrish realizes the woman is a spy. Penny accidentally outsmarts the men who are trying to catch spies on the base, including her brother David and Terry. Penny is disappointed, however, when she is not included in the spy's capture:

> Penny hung up the phone with great disappointment. Life seemed dull without her work of espionage. "It's all over," she said, flopping into a chair. "And just because I'm not in the army, I'm going to miss all the excitement at the end. Dad even said 'I'll tell you what I can'—and that may not be much."
>
> "But darling, you did catch them, you know." Carrol watched Bobby go off to relay the news to his mother, and added, "Think what it means to me, Penny, just one person. Suppose the Germans should be on the watch for our convoy. Why, it means everything to me! And think of all the other wives and mothers—think of Mums!"[5]

As the conversation continues, Penny clearly expresses a desire to be more actively involved in the war, perhaps in the Women's Army Corps or FBI. Carrol suggests that Penny enjoy her moment and leave war work to the men. The next scene involves Colonel Parrish and David sharing the exciting story about the capture and confession of the spy. For Penny, it seems involvement in the war is all or nothing—she wants to be involved in the action and excitement along with the men or not be involved at all. Carrol and Mrs. Parrish, on the other hand, are content to be army wives.

Usually the role of the women in the Parrish family is to support their men, including David and Colonel Parrish, who are sent to Europe. Very rarely, however, are the men in the stories hurt or killed, despite the fact that World War II "brought death to some 60 million people worldwide."[6] A military wife herself, Lambert would have been keenly aware of the sadness brought to many families who lost men during the war, but she protected the young people in her stories and her readers from these harsh realities.

Lambert's wartime books are also missing many of the details of women's lives on the home front. There is little rationing of goods, which was common practice during World War II. The Parrishes have all the consumer goods they need, many provided by Carrol, despite the fact that many goods were scarce during the war: "The Office of Price Administration regulated prices to control inflation and rationed such scarce commodities as gasoline, rubber, steel, shoes, coffee, sugar, and meat."[7] There are few references to Red Cross work; once Carrol mentions an appointment at the Red Cross. There is no sign of "Rosie the Riveter," the women who worked in factories as welders, shipbuilders, lumberjacks, and miners. In Lambert's fictional world, life goes on as normal, with the absence of some of the men. The women are patriotic and happy to belong to the army, and thus they sacrifice their men temporarily. This is the extent that war touches their lives.

In *Practically Perfect*, David Parrish returns home from war, ready to retire from the military. The end of the war, the atomic bombings of Hiroshima and Nagasaki, and the advent of the nuclear age are forgotten as David takes up farming at Gladstone, the estate his wife inherited from her father. Farming had become big business during the early 1940s: "Income derived from farming, which had lagged through the many years of low prices and overproduction, doubled and then doubled again."[8] David enters the postwar economy positioned to add to his family's wealth, while Carrol cares for their son.

Before the war is over, Penny begins her acting career on Broadway, where she meets her mentor and future husband, Josh MacDonald. A struggling director and producer, Josh is twelve years older than Penny, and he takes on the role of manager and father figure. As she prepares for a date with Josh as a publicity stunt in *Practically Perfect*, Penny tells her mother,

> "Josh mixes me up so," she complained to her reflection and Ma in the background. "Here I am, going out with him so he can treat me like some kind of a—a paper doll—the kind you cut and bend so it'll sit down to a pretend tea party, and then you'll go off and forget."
>
> "Josh never forgets you, not for one minute," Ma answered, flipping Penny's dress from its hanger. "Don't fool yourself. He's too interested in making a career for himself through you."[9]

Penny and her mother know the relationship is based on work. But Penny, who is falling in love with the older Josh, doesn't yet realize that he loves her. So she carries on acting as child to Josh's father figure:

> He was ordering a chicken sandwich and a glass of milk for her and she whispered, "Goodness, Josh, do I have to drink *milk*? Can't I have coffee or a coke?"

> But he shook his head. "You worked hard tonight," he answered, nod-
> ding the order to the waiter. "Little girls who work need nourishment."
> "Oh, me." Penny sighed and dared a look around her.[10]

Penny allows Josh to make decisions for her about what she will eat
and why she will eat it. Even though they aren't on an official date,
Josh flirts with Penny. The flirting is meant to make Penny look good
for photographers, and Josh hopes her picture will be published in the
newspaper. But all on her own, Penny accidentally attracts the attention of the entire room, including photographers, when she bumps into
family friend and military hero General Wainwright. "For a shy little
girl who doesn't want publicity," Josh teased when she came back, "you
certainly can walk right into it."[11] Penny's picture appears in the newspaper the next morning.

Even though Josh usually plays the role of father figure, Penny
breaks out of traditional gender roles at critical moments in their relationship. Penny decides they will marry after they declare their love for
each other. In a gender role reversal, it is Josh who is surprised and
happy to be chosen by Penny, not the other way around. After their
marriage, Penny retires from acting to raise their two children. In *The
Reluctant Heart*, she realizes Josh is unhappy. "That she was being selfish never entered her pretty head. That Josh missed the gay, enthusias-
tic, ambitious young actress he had married five years earlier just never
occurred to Penny until it was almost too late."[12] Penny reluctantly returns to work, demonstrating the struggles future generations of women
would experience while juggling work and family responsibilities, to
make her husband happy.

Lambert's stories came straight from her own life experiences as an
actress, a military wife, and a mother, but were no doubt purified for her
young readers. After all, dust jacket ads for "The Famous Janet Lambert
Books for Girls" proclaim, "Stories about teenagers . . . written specially
for teenagers." Lambert's stories were akin to the fantasy life found in
such 1940s bobby-soxer films as *The Bachelor and the Bobby-Soxer* and
the Corliss Archer movies starring a teenage Shirley Temple. Teen girls
loved the fantasy life portrayed in the pictures, including the "upper-
middle-class suburban life, parties, pretty clothes, indulgent parents,
[and] faithful and adoring boys next door."[13] Girls loved Penny Parrish's

wonderful fantasy life, too. Classical and Medieval scholar Anne B. Thompson fondly remembers Lambert's Parrish family stories: "[R]omantic novels by Lambert and others were important to me."[14]

But book critics have not been kind to Lambert. Richard S. Alm refers to Lambert's books, including the Parrish Family and Candy Kane series, as "inferior."[15] He argues that Candy and Penny are too simple because they like to help people and they want others to be happy. Young adult literature historian Michael Cart easily dismisses Lambert's books as escapist literature for girls. Cart suggests that teen romance novels of the era are merely pale imitations of the critically acclaimed *Seventeenth Summer*, first published by Maureen Daly in 1942.[16] Despite the contempt of male critics, Lambert's series books made a lasting impression on teenage girls, and the Parrish and Jordan family stories continued publishing through the next two decades. Another similar series, Beany Malone, by Lenora Mattingly Weber, was also popular with readers for nearly three decades.

Career Women and World War II

During World War II, girls' series books portrayed women in such careers as journalism and nursing. Sixteen-year-old Penny Parker, the creation of journalist and Stratemeyer Syndicate writer Mildred Wirt, continued her investigative journalism career. During the war, Penny helps the army capture crooks at an enemy shortwave station in *Voice from the Cave*, and she investigates an explosion at a war factory in *Signal in the Dark*. The series is firmly set in the 1940s: "There is frequent mention of rationing, munitions plants, and other incidents circa World War II, as well as allusions to specific amounts of money."[17] When Penny solves a case, she writes about it for her newspaper, the *Riverview Star*. Beverly Gray also continues her exciting journalism and publishing careers. In *Beverly Gray, Reporter*, she catches spies who try to steal military plans. During the war, Beverly becomes a government agent so she can catch more spies in *Beverly Gray's Adventure*. While the Penny Parker series ceased publication in the late 1940s, Beverly Gray continued her adventures until the mid-1950s.

Of course, stories about career nurses were particularly popular during World War II. While Helen Dore Boylston's Sue Barton nursing series continued through the 1940s, the stories focus on Sue's marriage and nursing career, rather than on the events of World War II. In contrast, Helen Wells's Cherry Ames series focuses on an independent, ambitious career nurse who joins the army. Although several other nursing series were published during the war years, including Gail Gardner, Nancy Naylor, Ann Bartlett, Penny Marsh, Nurse Blake, Nurse Merton, and Patty Lou, the Cherry Ames series remains the most beloved of the nursing series.

In *Cherry Ames, Student Nurse* and *Cherry Ames, Senior Nurse*, teenaged Cherry trains for a nursing career. Author Helen Wells was asked to write the nursing series for Grosset & Dunlap after Margaret Sutton, already known for her Judy Bolton series, failed to deliver with the Gail Gardner series. "Grosset was dissatisfied because Gail Gardner was not enough like Sue Barton; moreover, Sutton wanted to take a nurse's aide course so she could write informatively. Grosset did not feel this was necessary."[18] Sutton took her Gail Gardner nursing series to publisher Dodd Mead, while Helen Wells created Cherry Ames for Grosset & Dunlap. Wells introduces Cherry as a caring and ambitious young woman:

> Cherry wanted a profession of her own. More than that, she wanted to do vital work, work that the world urgently needs. She honest-to-goodness cared about people and she wanted to help them on a grand and practical scale.[19]

Named Charity after her grandmother, she is nicknamed Cherry because of her healthy, rosy red cheeks.[20] The early Cherry Ames books are pure propaganda, meant to encourage teen readers to become nurses. After her nursing training, Cherry joins the army in *Cherry Ames, Army Nurse*. Scholar Sally E. Parry observes:

> Three of the books from the series that focus on the war—*Cherry Ames, Army Nurse* (1944), *Cherry Ames, Chief Nurse* (1944), *and Cherry Ames, Flight Nurse* (1945)—are quite authentic in describing the training a new nurse must undergo before she is sent to help the military overseas.[21]

In *Cherry Ames, Army Nurse*, Cherry and her classmates go to Fort Herold for four weeks of basic army training. At the end of the story,

Cherry and her friends, Gwen Jones, Bertha Larsen, Josie Franklin, Ann Evans, Vivian Warren, Mai Lee, and Marie Swift, are sworn into office for the duration of the war plus six months. Cherry is sent to the Pacific with a new medicine for blackwater fever. While serving on a Pacific island, Cherry is asked to set up a makeshift hospital in the jungle in *Cherry Ames, Chief Nurse.*

Although Cherry does an excellent job, her superiors constantly question her judgment, intellect, and abilities throughout *Cherry Ames, Chief Nurse.* The military men don't approve of Cherry's feminine touches, including the white nurses uniforms worn on Sundays and a party hosted by the nurses. But Cherry knows she is special because she is female, and she knows nursing is a noble profession: "For Cherry knew that, in peace just as much as in war, the world needs brave and understanding girls in that most feminine, most humane, and most beloved of all professions."[22]

Although it is not clear why Cherry gives up the plum job of chief nurse, in the next book, she works as a flight nurse, helping evacuate injured U.S. soldiers from European war zones to Allied England. Throughout the series, independent and intelligent Cherry clashes with male authority figures. She finds that male doctors and military officers don't take her seriously:

> "Frankly, Lieutenant Ames, you are too young to have had much nursing experience. Moreover, your extreme youth and your—er—attractive appearance suggest that you may not be quite the right person for this most serious work. I ought to warn you that you will not find it—er—glamorous."
>
> Cherry suppressed a flare-up of anger. And then, suddenly, she felt hurt and belittled. "I assure you, sir," the words rushed out, "I am not looking for glamour. I am perfectly responsible and serious. Perhaps my appearance is misleading, sir."[23]

Later Cherry asks, "Oh, Major Pierce, how can I make myself older, uglier, and more unpopular?"[24] Cherry is aware that her age, gender, and femininity are not appreciated by her male superiors. In direct contradiction with her feminine and caring nature, however, she often breaks the rules to help her patients. This means she is frequently in trouble with such male authority figures as doctors and army officers.

Of course, it always turns out that Cherry is right and the male authorities are wrong. For instance, in *Cherry Ames, Chief Nurse*, Cherry and her brother Charlie suspect that a soldier was injured with a new kind of weapon. When Cherry reports her suspicions to Colonel Pillsbee's superiors, he berates her. But when the soldier recovers under Cherry's care and he confirms her suspicions, Cherry is awarded a citation, and Colonel Pillsbee praises her work. Parry suggests that the Cherry Ames series is subversive:

> The Cherry Ames series is somewhat subversive in that, although these types of authority are given lip service, when Cherry has to break regulations to help a sick Central American native or to investigate the curious psychological problems of a downed flier, she is usually demonstrated to be in the right. The authorities, be they doctors and/or military officers, sanction what Cherry has done only after the fact and . . . Cherry's innate good sense is rewarded.[25]

After Cherry breaks the rules, she realizes that the consequences of her actions could mean the loss of a job or dishonorable discharge from the army. She suffers from worry and guilt over the possible consequences of her actions. But readers know Cherry is right, and eventually, she is vindicated.

Although the focus is on Cherry's career, she is not immune to romance, but she is unlikely to marry any man during the war because she is dedicated to her job. Doctors and military officers regularly fall in love with her, but none of the wartime romances last. When Dr. Lex Upham proposes marriage in *Cherry Ames, Army Nurse*, she is horrified: "You . . . you can't propose to me in a hospital office! And anyhow, even though army nurses are permitted to marry, I don't know what to say. I don't even know," she wailed, "if I want to get married yet!"[26] She postpones her answer and is literally saved by the bell when the telephone rings with her orders to ship out to the Pacific immediately. Later, in *Cherry Ames, Flight Nurse*, Cherry is sad to learn Lex has married someone else, but she realizes she never loved him. Her friendship with pilot Wade Cooper, who clearly likes Cherry as more than a friend, helps her forget about Lex. Wade is more upset than Cherry when they must say goodbye at the end of *Cherry Ames, Flight Nurse*, but readers know that kind, caring Cherry will eventually find a husband, if and when she wants one.

But postwar books in the series feature Cherry's ongoing nursing career, rather than her search for a husband. In *Cherry Ames, Veterans' Nurse*, Cherry is surprised when her army enlistment ends. After much soul-searching, she decides not to reenlist but rather to seek new nursing opportunities outside the army. She works as a private duty nurse, a visiting nurse, a cruise nurse, and finally, in 1949 she ends up back at Spencer Hospital, where she took her training. After the war, Cherry takes up sleuthing more regularly as mystery becomes the focus of these career stories. The only mystery that remains unsolved is why Cherry changes jobs so frequently.

In 1949, the same year Cherry Ames returned to Spencer Hospital, Helen Dore Boylston resurrected beloved Nurse Sue Barton. In *Sue Barton, Neighborhood Nurse*, Sue questions her decision to give up her career, and she begins nursing people in her own neighborhood. Scholar Julia Hallam argues, however, that Sue's roles as nurse, wife, and mother are synonymous:

> Because Sue marries a doctor, the difference between work in the public sphere as a nurse and work in the private sphere as a wife is subsumed into the discourse of heterosexual relationships. The hospital becomes a metaphor for home life, with doctors as "fathers," nurses as "wives," and "mothers" and patients as "children."[27]

Sue decides that she must stop caring for the entire neighborhood when she learns she is pregnant with her fourth child. Sue later returns to working as a hospital nurse, while her doctor husband, Bill, recuperates from pneumonia and tuberculosis at a sanatorium in *Sue Barton, Staff Nurse*. Boylston justifies Sue's return to work with Bill's illness. In Bill's absence, Sue juggles her work and home responsibilities. *Sue Barton, Staff Nurse* ends with Bill's surprise return, which he secretly arranges with Kit so Sue will not resign her job at the hospital. He tells Kit, "Do you think it's a good idea for her to quit? She loves staff work, and she's been happy there. I could see it in her every time she came over here."[28] Bill concludes, however, the decision to continue working will be Sue's alone, and the end of the series leaves readers believing that Sue will continue to work after Bill's return. Hallam concludes, "Sue Barton manages to combine marriage and a career; through this juggling act, she symbolizes the possibility of institutional change for those becoming nurses in the future."[29] Boylston was apparently content to leave the Sue Barton series on this note.

In the postwar years, author Helen Wells also gave up her Cherry Ames nursing series so she could write for radio and television. Publisher Grosset & Dunlap wanted to continue the popular nursing series, so they hired literary agent and author Julie Tatham to write *Cherry Ames, Cruise Nurse*. Series fiction experts James D. Keeline and Kimberlee Keeline note, "The book was published under Helen Wells's name because the artwork for the covers had already been ordered and the books largely presold."[30] Tatham also took over the writing of another Wells series, Vicki Barr Flight Stewardess. Wells returned to both series in the mid-1950s, and she continued to write both series until they ceased publication in the 1960s.

The first book in the Vicki Barr series, *Silver Wings for Vicki*, was published in 1947. When twenty-year-old Vicki Barr is selected for training at the Federal Airlines Stewardess School, her parents agree to let her drop out of college. Petite, ash blonde Vicki wants to be independent: "Imagine not having to ask Dad for things. Being master of my fate and captain of my own pocketbook."[31] But being an independent woman in the late 1940s meant pursuing a career that was regarded as acceptable for women. The job of airline stewardess offered readers an approved career choice and, at the same time, exciting adventures in exotic locales:

> Vicki Barr was not able to pursue traditional "men's jobs" as her profession . . . but she did manage to control her fate and travel around the world on her own in a way that most young girls would not have imagined possible for themselves at the time the books were written.[32]

Like Cherry Ames, Vicki solves mysteries while she works. In *Silver Wings for Vicki*, she accidentally lands in the middle of an FBI jewel smuggling investigation, and she helps identify the smugglers among her passengers. By the end of the decade, Vicki had solved four mysteries in such exciting places as New Orleans and Mexico. Vicki also finds romance in her travels, but like Cherry Ames, she is more interested in her work than in romance. This is just as well, since stewardesses in the

Vicki Barr books are not allowed to marry. Scholar Kathleen R. Chamberlain notes, "None of the girls thinks to ask why business couldn't be carried out just as satisfactorily with married stewardesses."[33] Vicki accepts the rules and carries on with her work.

While male pilots provide mild romantic interests, they often act as big brothers or father figures to the young female stewardesses. In *Vicki Finds the Answer*, a pilot is described as "a hearty, comfortable, dependable man, one of the nicest of the 'big brother' pilots."[34] Bobbie Ann Mason suggests that, "The assumption is that Vicki's daddy wouldn't let her go gallivanting off into the blue unless there was such a comfortable male to take care of her."[35] Unlike Cherry Ames, Vicki accepts her subservient role to the men who are in charge of her big, exciting world.

Career girl Connie Blair, who begins with a brief modeling career and then moves into the advertising world, arrived in the late 1940s. The series was written by author Betty Cavanna, who was already known for her light teenage romance stories, including *Going on Sixteen* and *A Girl Can Dream*. Using the pseudonym Betsy Allen, she combined career and mystery in the Connie Blair series. In *The Clue in Blue*, Connie works as a clothes model at Campion's Department Store. She saves her beloved Aunt Bet's reputation and career when she captures thieves who are trying to frame her for stealing from the store.

In *The Riddle in Red*, Connie and her twin sister, Kit, postpone college after their father has a heart attack. While Kit manages the family hardware store in small the town of Meadowbrook, Connie gets a job as a receptionist at the advertising firm Reid and Renshaw in Philadelphia. Connie wants to be a career girl like Aunt Bet, who shares her apartment with Connie. According to Chamberlain, "Though Connie Blair starts out as a receptionist at her advertising agency, she eventually goes to art school, wins promotions in the art department, and gets plum assignments to do on her own."[36] In twelve books titled for a full palette of colors, Connie solves mysteries focusing on items important to women, including clothing, jewelry, and cosmetics. Sometimes Connie is accompanied on her adventures by her bland twin sister, who seems only to exist to show readers what a wonderful heroine they have in Connie.

Romance figures more prominently in the Connie Blair series than in the other career stories of the late 1940s, since their author was known for her romantic stories, and the series was criticized for its "boy of the book concept."[37] Since Connie dates a different boy in each book, none of the romances are serious, and she remains committed to her career. Critics agree that the Connie Blair series, like the Vicki Barr series, generally accepts and promotes sex role stereotypes for both men and women in the 1940s, but Chamberlain argues that the Connie Blair series questions these stereotypes directly:

> The series publishers obviously were not interested in reforming sex role stereotypes in the professions. They simply wanted to produce books that would appeal to adolescent girls. And just as obviously, the readers were interested in glamorous careers that could make exciting reading. Models, stewardesses, actresses, and nurses fit the bill well without requiring the readers to enter completely alien territory.[38]

Some career series, like Sue Barton and Cherry Ames, were more successful in challenging gender stereotypes. Of course, if any of the series were too subversive, they would not have been popular. Some authors, like Helen Dore Boylston, Helen Wells, and Julie Tatham, were able to create strong career women who were appealing to readers in an era when American women had more freedom and opportunity than ever before. The Sue Barton and Cherry Ames nursing series were more popular than other career series, even after the war ended, because the protagonists challenged the patriarchal hierarchy and were rewarded for it.

Mystery Series

Several popular mystery series from the 1930s, including Nancy Drew, Judy Bolton, Beverly Gray, and The Dana Girls, continued publishing in the 1940s. Less popular series, like Kay Tracey and Penny Parker, ceased publication before the end of the decade. While such new career girls as Cherry Ames, Vicki Barr, and Connie Blair were busy solving mysteries connected with their work, author and literary agent Julie Tatham was invited to create and write two new series for the Whitman Publishing Company. Whitman was looking for writers to produce fast-paced children's books that could be published cheaply. Although Tatham kept busy writing the Cherry Ames and Vicki Barr series in the late 1940s, she was keen to create her own series when the opportunity was presented to her. Both the Trixie Belden and Ginny Gordon series debuted in 1948, published under the author's maiden name, Julie Campbell.

Thirteen-year-old tomboy and amateur detective Beatrix "Trixie" Belden was introduced to readers in *The Secret of the Mansion*. Trixie lives on Crabapple Farm in Sleepyside-on-the Hudson, New York, with her parents and brothers, Brian, Mart, and Bobby. Trixie has blonde curly hair, blue eyes, and a quick temper. When she gets frustrated, she tugs on her blonde curls. Trixie likes horseback riding, and she wants to open her own detective agency when she grows up. In creating the Trixie Belden series, Tatham was interested in writing mystery stories that were different from other popular series. She declared, "I wanted Trixie to be different from Nancy Drew . . . I thought Nancy Drew books were poorly written and totally implausible."[39] Trixie is indeed very different from the older, more sophisticated Nancy Drew.

In the first book in the series, Trixie becomes best friends with her new neighbor, Madeleine "Honey" Wheeler, whose wealthy family moves into the Manor House next door. While Honey is more feminine than Trixie, she gets over her fear of nearly everything with Trixie's help, and she happily puts on a pair of jeans and follows her friend's lead in seeking mystery and adventure. The mystery in *The Secret of the Mansion* focuses on Jim Frayne, a young man Trixie and Honey find hiding in an old mansion near their homes. Jim has run away from his abusive stepfather, and he is searching for his uncle's fortune, supposedly hidden in the house. Jim runs away again before he learns he is heir to a fortune. In the second book in the series, *The Red Trailer Mystery*, Trixie and Honey find Jim and tell him about his inheritance. The Wheelers adopt Jim.

Trixie, Brian, Mart, Honey, and Jim form a club called the Bob-Whites of the Glen with their friends Diana Lynch and Dan Mangan. The Bob-Whites of the Glen get involved in community service projects, raising money for charity and the repair of their clubhouse. Somehow, even when they try to stay out of trouble, Trixie and Honey always find mysteries for the group to solve. While the group pairs off—Trixie with Jim, Diana with Mart, and Honey with Brian—romance plays a very small role in the series.

In 1948, Tatham also published the first book in the Ginny Gordon series, which was very similar to Trixie Belden. Trixie and Ginny are similar in looks and character. They both live in New York state and solve mysteries with the help of their friends. Fourteen-year-old Ginny lives in Harristown, where she forms a club called the Hustlers with her friends, John Blaketon, Lucy Tryon, and twins Whiz and Babs Reilly. In *Ginny Gordon and the Mystery of the Disappearing Candlesticks*, the Hustlers open a swap shop, where they sell second-hand goods. When two silver candlesticks mistakenly donated to the swap shop are stolen, Ginny and the Hustlers must find them or their swap shop will be out of business. It is puzzling why Tatham wrote two very similar series and why Whitman published both series at the same time. While Ginny Gordon only lasted until the mid-1950s, Trixie Belden continued publishing for several decades.

The Trixie Belden series survived because young Trixie was the antithesis of the older, more sophisticated girl sleuths: "If Nancy Drew was the ideal that we could never attain, and Judy Bolton was our beloved sister who tried but was never quite able to change the world, then Trixie Belden was us."[40] Despite its appeal, Trixie Belden didn't really become popular until the 1950s, when it gained series status.

Romantic family stories, career series, and mysteries were all popular genres for girls' series books during the 1940s. While life during World War II is softened in these stories, the need for working women was evident in series like Cherry Ames, even if the stories were not always realistic. While it may be surprising that career stories continued to be published after the war, it's not surprising that mysteries became more popular again. With the excitement and adventure of the war over, young fictional career women did more sleuthing to remain popular with readers. Although many of the series supported traditional gender roles, such series as Nancy Drew, Sue Barton, Cherry Ames, and Trixie Belden were popular with teen readers because they sometimes dared to challenge the patriarchal structure of American society, both during and after the war.

Notes

1. John M. Murrin, Paul E. Johnson, James M. McPherson, Alice Fahs, and Gary Gerstle, *Liberty, Equality, and Power: A History of the American People* (Belmont, CA: Thomson Wadsworth, 2006), 935.

2. Lucy Rollin, *Twentieth-Century Teen Culture by the Decades* (Westport, CT: Greenwood, 1999), 103.

3. Rollin, *Twentieth-Century Teen Culture by the Decades*, 103.

4. Grace Palladino, *Teenagers: An American History* (New York: Basic-Books, 1996), 104.

5. Janet Lambert, *Up Goes the Curtain* (New York: Grosset & Dunlap, 1946), 89.

6. Murrin et al., *Liberty, Equality, and Power*, 960.

7. Murrin et al., *Liberty, Equality, and Power*, 957.

8. Murrin et al., *Liberty, Equality, and Power*, 963.

9. Janet Lambert, *Practically Perfect* (New York: Grosset & Dunlap, 1947), 33–34.

10. Lambert, *Practically Perfect*, 35.

11. Lambert, *Practically Perfect*, 36.

12. Janet Lambert, *The Reluctant Heart* (New York: Grosset & Dunlap, 1950), dust jacket blurb.

13. Rollin, *Twentieth-Century Teen Culture by the Decades*, 140.

14. Anne B. Thompson, "Rereading Fifties Teen Romance: Reflections on Janet Lambert," *The Lion and the Unicorn*, 29.3 (2005): 374.

15. Richard S. Alm, "The Glitter and the Gold," *The English Journal*, 44.6 (1955): 316.

16. Michael Cart, *From Romance to Realism: 50 Years of Growth and Change in Young Adult Literature* (New York: HarperCollins, 1996), 23–24.

17. Society of Phantom Friends, *The Girls' Series Companion* (Rheem Valley, CA: SynSine, 1997), 434.

18. Society of Phantom Friends, *The Girls' Series Companion*, 170.

19. Helen Wells, *Cherry Ames, Student Nurse* (New York: Grosset & Dunlap, 1943), 6.

20. John Axe, *All about Collecting Girls' Series Books* (Grantsville, MD: Hobby House, 2002), 127.

21. Sally E. Parry, "You Are Needed, Desperately Needed!: Cherry Ames in World War II," in *Nancy Drew and Company: Culture, Gender, and Girls' Series*, ed. Sherrie A. Inness (Bowling Green, OH: Bowling Green State University Popular Press, 1997), 135.

22. Helen Wells, *Cherry Ames, Chief Nurse* (New York: Grosset & Dunlap, 1944), 13.

23. Wells, *Cherry Ames, Chief Nurse*, 9.

24. Wells, *Cherry Ames, Chief Nurse*, 72.

25. Parry, "You Are Needed, Desperately Needed!" 139.

26. Helen Wells, *Cherry Ames, Army Nurse* (New York: Grosset & Dunlap, 1944), 203.

27. Julia Hallam, "Nursing an Image: The Sue Barton Career Novels," in *Image and Power: Women in Fiction in the Twentieth Century*, ed. Sarah Sceats and Gail Cunningham (London: Longman, 1996), 93.

28. Helen Dore Boylston, *Sue Barton, Staff Nurse* (Boston: Little, Brown and Company, 1952), 194.

29. Hallam, "Nursing an Image," 101.

30. James D. Keeline and Kimberlee Keeline, "Trixie Belden: Schoolgirl Shamus" (paper presented at the Popular Culture Association National Conference, Lake Buena Vista, Florida, April 10, 1998), www.keeline.com/Trixie_Belden.pdf (accessed July 26, 2007).

31. Helen Wells, *Silver Wings for Vicki* (New York: Grosset & Dunlap, 1947), 30.

32. Axe, *All about Collecting Girls' Series Books*, 143.

33. Kathleen R. Chamberlain, "Every Girls' Ambition: Careers in Girls' Series Fiction, 1940–1970," *Dime Novel Round-Up*, 60.6 (1991): 108.

34. Helen Wells, *Vicki Finds the Answer* (New York: Grosset & Dunlap, 1947), 32.

35. Bobbie Ann Mason, *The Girl Sleuth* (Athens: University of Georgia Press, 1995), 113.

36. Chamberlain, "Every Girl's Ambition," 110.

37. Society of Phantom Friends, *The Girls' Series Companion*, 107.

38. Chamberlain, "Every Girl's Ambition," 109.

39. "Julie Tatham," in *Something about the Author: Volume 80*, ed. Kevin S. Hile (New York: Gale Research, 1995), 231.

40. Kate Emburg, foreword to *Schoolgirl Shamuses, Inc.*, by Melanie Knight (Rheem Valley, CA: SynSine, 1998), 1.

6

Romances and Revisions:
The Junior Novel and the New Nancy Drew

In the 1950s, romance series reigned supreme in the form of the junior novel. Following the tremendous success of Maureen Daly's romantic *Seventeenth Summer* in the previous decade, publishers produced mass market romance novels for teens. While Janet Lambert's romantic Parrish Family and Jordan Family stories remained popular with readers through the 1950s, such authors as Rosamund Du Jardin and Anne Emery wrote about teen girls who worried about being popular, dating, college, and marriage. Lambert's stories featured Penny Parrish's younger sister, Tippy, along with Alice, Susan, and Bitsy Jordan. Rosamund Du Jardin wrote lighter, humorous romantic stories focusing on sisters Tobey and Midge Heydon, twins Pam and Penny Howard, and Marcy Rhodes. Anne B. Thompson contends,

> No one who has ever read a teen novel for girls written at this time will fail to recognize their salient characteristics: the focus on and idealization of domesticity and family life; the lack of serious problems; and the absence of specific historical or cultural context.[1]

While Thompson is correct in stating that most 1950s romances generally focus on domesticity and family, many series display a definite historical and cultural context. Other series diverge from the focus on domesticity and family, instead focusing on the growth and development of the female protagonist. Anne Emery's Pat Marlowe and Dinny Gordon series, published in the late 1950s, are quite different from the happily-ever-after romantic stories written by her contemporaries.

In a decade when young women were encouraged to become housewives and mothers, career series remained absurdly popular with teen readers. In the post–World War II era, such career series as Cherry Ames, Vicki Barr, Connie Blair, and Beverly Gray were considered more mystery than career stories, although the young protagonists still had healthy careers. Mystery series reigned supreme, for example Nancy Drew, The Dana Girls, Kay Tracey, Judy Bolton, and Trixie Belden.

The most important event to take place in girls' series publishing, however, was the revision of the Nancy Drew series, which began in 1958. Harriet Adams, president of the Stratemeyer Syndicate, was forced by her publisher to revise the Nancy Drew books. Although Adams did not completely understand complaints about racial stereotypes in the Stratemeyer Syndicate's books, she bowed to pressure from Grosset & Dunlap to remove outdated prejudices from their most popular series, including Nancy Drew and The Hardy Boys. The revision finally gave Adams the opportunity to change Mildred Wirt's Nancy Drew into someone more like herself. The new Nancy Drew became a role model for generations of teens.

The Junior Novel and Romance Series

During the 1950s, Janet Lambert continued her series about the Parrish and Jordan families, focusing on Tippy Parrish and her friends from the Jordan family. Living in postwar Germany with her parents in *Little Miss Atlas*, Tippy misses Peter Jordan. When she meets young Lieutenant Ken Prescott, however, Tippy falls in love. She has always wanted to marry an army officer:

> "Why, of course I'd marry an army officer." Tippy sat up again and watched the road, too, the delightful, lovely road and countryside. "I couldn't marry anyone else," she said simply. "Penny did, and David got out of the army to manage Carrol's big estate, but I'm army clear through."[2]

Tippy returns to the United States with her parents when her father retires from the military, while Ken is sent to Korea. In the early 1950s, the United States joined South Korea in war against Soviet-supported Communist North Korea. Lambert firmly anchors her story in the early 1950s, sending Ken to Korea to fight communism. While Ken is on leave, he gets engaged to Tippy in *Don't Cry, Little Girl*, but he must return to duty. Tragedy strikes the Parrish family when Ken is killed in combat. Tippy is visiting her brother Bobby and friend Peter Jordan at West Point Academy when news arrives. Colonel Parrish can't bear to tell Tippy the bad news, so he enlists Peter to do it for him. Young Peter, who loves Tippy dearly, knows it's his duty to tell her about Ken's death, and he tries to break the terrible news to her gently: "I love you," he repeated, "and I'd rather die than hurt you. But I have to, darling. Put your head against me because I have to tell you, Tippy, it's Ken."[3] Tippy goes into shock, and young Peter flails around, trying to figure out what he should do next. He is rescued by Tippy's brother-in-law, Josh, who arrives to take them home. Anne B. Thompson recounts her reaction to Ken's death:

> I could not understand when I first read the series at age thirteen or fourteen, why lovely, romantic *older* Ken had to die, to be replaced, eventually, in Tippy's affections by boring hometown *same-age* Peter. This kind of thing was not supposed to happen in this kind of book, and though, of course, I would not have put it this way at the time, I felt that Lambert's contract with the reader, that is, me, had been betrayed. Rereading the books I'm still angry about Ken dying.[4]

Perhaps by the early 1950s, Lambert decided it was important to include the reality of war in her romantic stories. Since the Korean War was the second military conflict to take place during her series, it may have seemed unrealistic that everyone in the stories survives two wars. In *Rainbow after Rain*, Tippy agrees to marry faithful Peter, who is beginning his military career. Once she decides to get married, Tippy wants the wedding to take place right away, afraid something bad might happen to Peter if they wait. But her family convinces her to have the big wedding of her dreams, which takes place in *Welcome Home, Mrs. Jordan*.

Before Tippy becomes a married woman, her family and boyfriends treat her like a child. Ken calls her "Cherub," while Peter calls her

"Childie." Tippy regards army officers Ken and Peter as father figures, rather than lovers. At one point in *Little Miss Atlas*, Tippy is so unhappy in Germany that her parents and Ken decide she should go home. Ken is not even her fiancé yet, but since he is an older man who cares for Tippy, he assists her parents in decisions about her welfare. Colonel Parrish, retired from the army, surrenders responsibility for his daughter to Peter when he asks him to tell her about Ken's death. Even Tippy's brother-in-law, Josh MacDonald, whom she had a crush on before he married her sister Penny, rushes in like the knight in shining armor (in this case, in a car) to rescue Tippy and Peter at a crucial moment.

Tippy's boyfriends are portrayed as father figures, instead of the sex-crazed teenage boys they would likely have been in real life. This phenomenon is seen in other teen romance series from the 1950s. For instance, college student Brad Kenyon befriends Dinny when he is invited to the Gordon household to meet her older sister, Roxie, in *Dinny Gordon, Sophomore*. Brad remains a distant yet constant presence in Dinny's life, encouraging her interest in archaeology as a career. Brad also gives Dinny sage advice about friendship and dating, and she listens to him because he is a more experienced, older man. Part way through reading the series, I wondered why Brad was still hanging around when it was clear he wasn't interested in Roxie. Then I realized he was waiting for Dinny to finish high school so they could date. *Dinny Gordon, Senior* ends as she prepares to leave for a trip to Europe and the Middle East, wondering why she feels like she is forgetting something. When a telegram from Brad arrives wishing her well and is signed "Love, Brad," Dinny is ready to go, assured that Brad will be waiting for her.

Other series also demonstrate the father figure and child relationship among young couples. In the Pat Marlowe series, despite their plans to marry, older Tim breaks up with Pat partly because he is frustrated by her inability to save money and her desire to buy things he believes are frivolous. In Rosamund Du Jardin's Pam and Penny Howard series, Penny goes steady with strong, authoritative Mike Bradley for several years before they marry in *Double Wedding*.

Unlike other junior novels of the decade, Thompson argues that Lambert's Tippy Parrish books are solidly grounded in the history and culture of the early 1950s:

The events and the time period of [*Little Miss Atlas*; *Miss America*; *Don't Cry, Little Girl*; and *Rainbow After Rain*] conform to the real historical events, which form their background: the rebuilding of Germany after World War II, the beginning of the Cold War, and the invasion of South Korea.[5]

Thompson contends, "[t]his makes them different from the context-free qualities of many 1950s romances."[6] Other 1950s romance series show historical and cultural context, although on a smaller scale than Lambert's books. In Rosamund Du Jardin's Tobey and Midge Heydon series, Tobey's friend, Dick Allen, joins the Navy in *Boy Trouble*. Pam and Penny Howard meet several young men at Harwood College who fought in battle, although Du Jardin is vague about which war. There is generally no indication of an actual war, other than mention of the draft, and no information about contemporary world events is offered in most junior novels.

Instead, Rosamund Du Jardin's romance series, including Pam and Penny Howard, Marcy Rhodes, and Tobey and Midge Heydon, are light and innocent stories of first loves and first kisses. "Pam and Penny Howard are identical twins with different personalities, a concept that has been the backbone of many popular series," observes the Society of Phantom Friends.[7] In *Double Date*, Pam and Penny move to suburban Glenhurst with their mother and grandmother. Shy, quiet Penny decides not to copy her vivacious, popular twin anymore, so she makes new friends and joins the high school newspaper. Before long, the twins are vying for the affections of Mike Bradley, who often hangs out in the Howard's living room listening to records with Pam and Penny. At the end of the story, Penny is voted prom queen because she created a scheme to ensure that all the senior girls had dates for the prom, making her more popular than her sister. At the end of the story, Penny agrees to go steady with Mike, and they share sweet kisses.

The other three books in the series focus on the twins' life at Harwood College, where Pam continues to date many boys. When Pam falls for slick Cade Venner in *Double Feature*, Penny and Mike are worried, and they introduce her to student and farmer Jeff Moore. Like David Parrish, Jeff sees a bright future in farming, and he saves money to buy land and machinery. When Jeff rescues Pam after Cade abandons her on a date, Pam realizes, "Jeff was a rock to cling to, strength when you needed it, understanding with no questions asked. Jeff was someone quite wonderful."[8] In *Double Wedding*, the twins graduate from college and have a double wedding, with Penny marrying Mike and Pam marrying Jeff.

Leading up to the wedding, Penny doubts that Mike still loves her when he breaks dates and doesn't have time for her. Penny is relieved to learn Mike has been spending all his free time writing a book, rather than dating other women. Pam, on the other hand, is getting used to the idea of living on a farm in the country:

> Oh, she would have adjustments to make when she and Jeff were married, there would be much to learn. She might be pretty inefficient at first in many of the duties that would devolve on her as the wife of a farmer. But Jeff would be patient with her shortcomings, Pam knew.[9]

While Penny settles down early in the series with Mike, it takes Pam longer to find a mature relationship that will lead to marriage. There is no doubt, however, that marriage will be the twins' fate. Since teens across the United States were dating, going steady, and preparing to get married right out of high school or college, it was natural that Du Jardin's characters marry when they finished college. In the years after World War II, young adults were anxious to settle down in the new suburbs and raise children. Historian John M. Murrin and colleagues note, "Daily life in the suburbs was structured by a broad pattern of 'separate spheres': a public sphere of work and politics dominated by men and a private sphere of housework and child care reserved for women."[10] It would be another decade before Betty Friedan would describe the despair felt by many young housewives in *The Feminine Mystique*. Like other young women in the 1950s, Pam and Penny plan to stay in the private sphere, although when their mother and stepfather suggest that they get summer jobs before the wedding so they won't miss their fiancés, they readily agree:

> "Besides," Ty added, "I think it's good for anyone to have the experience of working. The regular hours, the responsibility, give you some grasp of the mechanics of earning a living. It will make you better wives, more capable of understanding your husbands' problems, too."[11]

Everyone seems to have forgotten that Mrs. Howard ran her own business with her daughters' help before she remarried. Du Jardin makes it very clear that careers are for men, but it is alright for women to work at temporary jobs. It is Mike, not Penny, who lands a job and a book contract before their wedding. In an effort to find redeeming qualities in Du Jardin's Pam and Penny Howard series, Cecile Magaliff notes, "the author points out the need for education and has the twins wait until their boyfriends have finished their college education before they marry."[12] Education is more important for young men. Girls are only considered grown-up when they understand their place in the world, college degree or not. Pam eventually realizes, "When you loved someone, it wasn't important where you lived, so long as he was there to help you adjust yourself to his background. Penny had known that from the beginning. Pam had taken a while to learn."[13]

While popular culture portrayed women as wives and mothers, by the end of the 1950s, nearly 40 percent of married mothers worked outside the home. Women worked in limited, gender segregated jobs: "Virtually all of the nation's nurses, telephone operators, secretaries, and elementary school teachers were women."[14] Women were not well paid, since men earned enough money to support a whole family. In the Pam and Penny Howard and the Tobey and Midge Heydon series, it is assumed that the girls will marry, have children, and keep house. Even Mrs. Howard and her mother, who are portrayed as independent women, both remarry. When Tobey Heydon's mother visits her older daughter in *Class Ring*, Tobey is left in charge of the household. In a hilarious series of events, her father assists her with the housework by writing a schedule and building shelves to store pots and pans, rather than actually helping her with the work. Tobey refers to the schedule as a "terrific headache"[15] and "a hated enemy."[16] When Tobey gets sick, Mr. Heydon takes over the duties on the schedule, and he realizes how much work is involved in keeping house. After he trips over his cleaning kit and injures his back, he hires a housekeeper to help until his wife returns. While their efforts at housekeeping are humorously portrayed, the message that only a married woman knows how to properly cook and keep house is very clear.

Like Pam and Penny Howard, Tobey eventually marries her long-time boyfriend, Brose Gilman, and the series shifts to the romances of younger sister Midge. Marcy Rhodes, on the other hand, gets a marriage proposal before she is out of high school. Instead of marrying, Marcy continues to date several boys. This romantic series ends with *Senior Prom*, when Marcy has trouble deciding who should take her to the dance. In the end, she makes the right choice, dating the safe boy next door, Rick, rather than wild Bruce, who is involved in a crash in his yellow convertible on prom night. In sum, "Du Jardin's girls are happy, social creatures who make friends easily, laugh a good deal, and enjoy themselves."[17]

"In Anne Emery, the teenaged reader has a novelist of considerable merit," critic Richard S. Alm commends.[18] Anne Emery's stories differ from other junior novels of the era, dealing with teen love more realistically than romantically. Pat Marlowe certainly expects to marry her boyfriend, Tim, but it all falls apart in *First Love Farewell*. Even after they break up, Pat still believes they will be married, but she realizes that Tim doesn't share her interest in the theater, and he expects her to give up her interests for him. Mrs. Marlowe reassures Pat that she can survive on her own:

> "I knew you were cutting out a lot of things that made you an interesting person," her mother said. "You depended too much on someone else. Never let yourself need anyone again the way you thought you needed Tim, Pat. It kills your personality."[19]

In a message distinctly different from the other romance series popular at the time, Pat realizes that true love should support her and let her grow as a person rather than destroy her. "When she met love again it would give her something instead of taking it away."[20] Pat plans to pursue her passion for the theater and make new friends before she falls in love again. In another Emery series, *Dinny Gordon, Freshman* tries to avoid dating. Dinny doesn't like any of the boys she knows, and she's more interested in planning her future career as an archaeologist, but many of Dinny's friends don't understand why she doesn't want to date. Unlike Dinny, many protagonists in 1950s junior novels are ready to go steady.

Although it was commonly known that going steady also meant teens were involved in sexual activity, teen romances didn't acknowledge anything beyond kissing. But Alfred C. Kinsey's study *Sexual Behavior in the Human Female*, published in 1953, found that many teen girls engaged in all sorts of sexual activity. But there was a double standard for white middle-class teens, the very audience of the romantic junior novels, with boys expected to be sexually active and girls expected to refrain from sex. Teen culture historian Lucy Rollin argues, "Kinsey had revealed that the stereotype of the virginal, innocent teen girl was a fantasy, and that even the stereotype of the home-loving, faithful wife might be suspect."[21] The junior novel, along with other series books aimed at teen readers during the 1950s remained in fantasyland as far as teen sexuality was concerned.

Instead, junior novels were light, easy reading. Cecile Magaliff suggests, "Their appeal apparently lies in the fact that they were all so positive. No great tragedies befall the heroines. They all wear nice clothes. They live in nice houses. They go through such nice adventures."[22] Librarian Margaret A. Edwards explains why teenage girls liked the junior novels:

> [A]t her age nothing is more important than a feeling of social security (not the government kind), and the best of these teenage stories, slight as they are, give her understanding of her peers and of herself and help smooth the road to happiness. They also develop a genuine love of reading [that] remains long after the girl outgrows this interest in stories of first love.[23]

Although Edwards understands the appeal of these books, she describes such book titles as *Boy Trouble*, *Double Date*, and *Going Steady* as "nauseous."[24] The critics gave light praise for these innocent stories of first loves, noting that the books were both "superficial"[25] and "wholesome.[26] Novelist Bobbie Ann Mason, who read a few junior novels growing up, distinguishes them from earlier girls' series books: "In the series books I see the sources of my dreams, while in the junior novel I see the conventional female role against which I rebelled from the very beginning."[27]

Career Series

While career series like Cherry Ames, Vicki Barr, Connie Blair, and Beverly Gray continued publishing in the 1950s, these popular career girls attracted readers because they had exciting adventures and because they solved mysteries while they worked. In correspondence with novelist Bobbie Ann Mason in the early 1970s, Cherry Ames and Vicki Barr author Helen Wells argued that mysteries were more profitable for publishers than other series genres: "My two series were primarily mystery stories because this is what Grosset and Dunlap wanted. A market existed, and still exists, for juvenile mysteries. The reason is as crass as that."[28]

Cherry Ames worked in mundane places like doctors' offices, rest homes, and hospitals, along with more exotic locales, like a dude ranch, a girls' summer camp, and a boarding school. But wherever Cherry went, she solved mysteries, like robberies and kidnappings. Her mysteries were not as exciting, however, as those she encountered when she served in World War II. Cherry's military service is rarely mentioned since it dated the stories. After the war, Cherry becomes ageless, moving from one job to another. She travels around the United States, visiting Kentucky, Arizona, Pennsylvania, and New York City. Cherry finds several jobs near her hometown of Hilton, Illinois, including *Cherry Ames at Hilton Hospital*.

While Cherry solves mysteries closer to home, Vicki Barr Air Stewardess continues to fly around the world solving mysteries. "While Cherry must constantly change jobs to pursue mysteries that conflict with her career, Vicki's mysteries are a natural outgrowth of her exciting job, and layovers give her plenty of time to track clues."[29] Vicki visits Hawaii, Canada, Alaska, Florida, New York City, and Chicago. In *Peril over the Airport*, published in 1953, pilot Bill Avery teaches Vicki to fly a plane. Book collector John Axe contends, "it appeared that [Vicki] would become a pilot, but somebody must have decided . . . girl readers would like her better if she retained the perceived glamour of a stewardess."[30] Moreover, Axe argues, "Vicki learns to fly a plane and is never quite the same again. Somehow, being a stewardess just is not enough anymore."[31] The series continues, however, with an unfulfilled Vicki for another decade.

While Julie Tatham wrote both the Cherry Ames and Vicki Barr series in the early 1950s, Helen Wells returned to write both series by the mid-1950s. Perhaps such perceptive readers as John Axe noticed a change in Vicki because the series changed writers. Tatham admitted that she purposely gave Cherry and Vicki lots of boyfriends: "My philosophy is to play the field. I couldn't tolerate this going steady stuff.

My heroines were plenty attractive. They had lots of beaux."[32] By increasing the amount of light romance in the series, Tatham offered teen readers something different from the romantic junior novels with her combination of career, mystery, and romance.

Betty Cavanna, known for her popular junior novels *Going on Sixteen* and *Paintbox Summer*, continued her Connie Blair career series under the pen name Betsey Allen until 1958. Connie's job as an advertising executive allows her and twin Kit to travel farther than Vicki Barr, solving mysteries in Mexico and the Caribbean. The twins encounter a perfumed ghost, search for a missing mink coat, find a stolen brooch, investigate a silver shop, discover missing porcelain figurines, and attend a cooking contest. Cavanna actually had a friend write *The Mystery of the Ruby Queens*, the last book in the series, because she was tired of writing series books. Perhaps Cavanna tired of searching for suitable adventures for the very feminine Blair twins. Helen Wells once described the limitations of writing girls' series books: "It's like writing in a straitjacket—or on a tiny canvas with only three colors to work with."[33]

Despite the limitations of the girls' series genre, author Clair Blank continued to write the Beverly Gray mystery series until 1955, when Grosset & Dunlap abruptly cancelled the series. *Beverly Gray's Surprise* is a shorter story, focusing on one mystery rather than a series of adventures, like previous books in the series. In this last story, Beverly is still a reporter at the *Herald Tribune* newspaper. She is engaged to Larry, and at the beginning of the story, Beverly attends the wedding of good friend Lois and her former beau Jim. After Beverly solves a robbery and absolves her friend, Mike McKay, of wrongdoing, the story ends with signs the series will continue. The real surprise for Beverly, and likely for author Clair Blank, was the cancellation of the series.

While Beverly Gray and Connie Blair ceased publication during the 1950s, Cherry Ames and Vicki Barr carried on, choosing careers over marriage.

Mystery Series

Popular Stratemeyer Syndicate mystery series like Nancy Drew and The Dana Girls continued publishing through the 1950s. The Stratemeyer Syndicate's Kay Tracey series, originally published from 1934 to

1942, was revised and reissued twice in the 1950s, first by Doubleday and Company's Garden City Books in 1951 and then later by Books, Inc., at the end of the decade. Only the first book in the series, *The Secret of the Red Scarf*, was substantially revised for reissue. In the 1951 edition, Kay and her friends help an amnesiac find his sister, and she saves their inheritance from an evil guardian. The rest of the titles in the Kay Tracey series were reissued, and the order of the titles was shifted around.

Revisions of Stratemeyer Syndicate series continued in 1958, when Nancy Drew and The Hardy Boys publisher Grosset & Dunlap requested updates to both popular series. For a decade, Grosset & Dunlap had received letters from parents who objected to the prejudice and racism in the books, which often featured stereotypical Jewish and African American characters. The publisher believed it was time to eliminate these outmoded stereotypes in the post–World War II, early Civil Rights era. Harriet Adams, president of the Stratemeyer Syndicate, did not completely understand why it was necessary to revise her popular series. Biographer Melanie Rehak suggests, "[I]t was not the first time that Harriet's genteel manners failed to cover the racism so typical of her generation and class."[34] In a letter to her sister, Adams wrote, "Grosset and Dunlap decided that these books were to be instantly revised because . . . the stories [were] antiquated and not in line with acceptable reading material for today's children."[35] Since revising the series was necessary for the Stratemeyer Syndicate's survival, Adams did what her publishers wanted.

By the mid-1950s, Adams was writing the Nancy Drew books rather than hiring ghostwriters. Adams did the revisions to the original books herself, which included adding more action and shortening the stories and, in some cases, writing whole new plots. Since Adams had trouble understanding the problems with the stereotypical portrayals of Jewish and African American characters, she simply eliminated these characters in the revised books, whitewashing Nancy's world.

Significantly, Nancy was completely transformed in the revisions. The new Nancy Drew, introduced in 1959, had titian rather than blonde hair. She was now eighteen years old because the driving age had gone up in the United States, and she drove a blue convertible instead of a roadster. After years of battling with Stratemeyer Syndicate writer

Mildred Wirt, Adams finally had the chance to make Nancy her own creation. "The girl, who Adams thought was 'too bold and bossy,' became more decorous, more like Harriet Adams and less like Mildred Wirt," report Carole Kismaric and Marvin Heiferman. "It was Adams's smartest move—or the worst decision she ever made, according to die-hard fans of the 'classic' books—to undertake the series' major overhaul, an eighteen-year commitment."[36] Revising the Stratemeyer Syndicate's most popular series was essential to the survival of the company, and in changing Nancy Drew, Adams ensured the fictional teen's popularity for several more decades. To survive, however, "Nancy went from being an inspiring mythical character to a rather ordinary teenage girl."[37] Adams's version of Nancy Drew was the perfect 1950s teen icon:

> Her larger-than-life mystique began to evaporate just as American women, who'd worked at men's jobs in factories during World War II, were being forced back into their homes, sealed off the from the complex realities of cold-war life, confined to ponder the mysteries of homemaking and the jobs of being good wives and perfect mothers.[38]

Nevertheless, for millions of teen readers through the next several decades, the new Nancy Drew created by Adams became a feminist icon. Even the diluted Nancy had more freedom, independence, and adventures than most readers could ever imagine.

For readers who didn't like the new Nancy Drew or her sister sleuths Kay Tracey or The Dana Girls, other mystery series were still available. Margaret Sutton's Judy Bolton series carried on, featuring Judy as housewife and amateur detective. Judy's husband Peter is a professional detective, working with the FBI. Judy's role as the wife of an FBI agent is clearly defined:

> My duties as the wife of an FBI agent were made clear to me when we were in Washington. I'm supposed to be a good housewife, with home and family my chief concern. I can keep pets and raise flowers and conduct myself like a model citizen, but never, no never, may I get myself involved in any of your assignments.[39]

Nevertheless, Judy searches for ghosts, thieves, kidnappers, missing children, and runaways, and she often accidentally solves Peter's cases for him. Judy is more interested in detecting crime than keeping house. Although Judy seeks adventure, she is not as independent or brave as Nancy Drew. For example, in *The Forbidden Chest*, she follows a boy she believes is a runaway, ending up on a train traveling across the United States. Judy is nervous not knowing where she is going, and she anxiously awaits Peter's telegrammed instructions. When she finally meets up with Peter again, she cries and falls into his arms. Fans of the series suggest that Judy Bolton seems more realistic than the Stratemeyer Syndicate heroines because "she has all [the] emotions and insecurities of a real girl."[40]

Julie Tatham's younger teen sleuths Trixie Belden and Ginny Gordon offered a change from such older girl sleuths as Nancy Drew and Judy Bolton. While the Ginny Gordon mysteries ended in 1956, Trixie Belden continued her adventures with her friends in the countryside of New York state. Although it got off to a slow start, the Trixie Belden series was sold by dimestore chains, and it gradually gained an audience. Trixie and the Bob-Whites of the Glen find missing runaways and diamond thieves, expose an extortion scheme, and catch a poacher. In the last book published in the 1950s, *The Mystery in Arizona* finds Trixie solving her first mystery away from home. The BWG's are working as waiters, maids, and dishwashers for Di's uncle, whose dude ranch employees have gone missing, and it's up to Trixie to find out what happened to the missing employees. Kate Emburg notes that the series was appealing because impulsive, impatient Trixie seemed more real than the older, more glamorous girl detectives:

> It was okay to be a tomboy like Trixie. It was okay, even preferable, to grow up having to pull weeds and babysit, rather than live in a mansion like Honey Wheeler. It was okay to think of being a detective as a real goal, not a silly fantasy. We didn't have to be rich, beautiful, or ladylike to achieve our dreams.[41]

After writing the first six books in the series, Julie Tatham decided to give up writing for young readers at the peak of her career to practice Christian Science. Whitman, her publisher, was determined to carry on with the series, and the pen name Kathryn Kenny was created. As the series creator, Tatham fought with publisher Whitman over who owned the characters, finally winning royalties for the use of her characters when the series continued without her.[42] Several writers were hired to write the series during the next twenty-five years. Of the beloved series she created and abandoned, Tatham stated in an interview, "Whitman had the intelligence to realize that if series books were written by good writers they could contribute a lot toward teaching the kids to read. And I don't mean learning to read. I mean *loving* to read."[43]

While on the surface it seems that the romantic junior novels, career stories, and mysteries were different kinds of books, all three genres had in common the element of mystery. While girl sleuths in both career and mystery stories found missing jewels, solved robberies, and searched for missing children, teen readers sought to solve other mysteries that baffled them—the secrets of dating, love, and romance. The romantic junior novels, which promoted domesticity and family life, were appealing because they explained parts of the mysteries of love and romance. As the 1950s came to a close, however, girls' series heroines were going in different directions. While the protagonists of some junior novels began thinking about college and careers, series focusing on young women with careers were fading. Most importantly, the revised Nancy Drew was a shadow of her former sassy self. Nevertheless, the new Nancy Drew would push other beloved series out of the market, and she would go on to become the most popular teen heroine of the century.

Notes

1. Anne B. Thompson, "Rereading Fifties Teen Romance: Reflections on Janet Lambert," *The Lion and the Unicorn*, 29.3 (2005): 375.

2. Janet Lambert, *Miss America*, (New York: Grosset & Dunlap, 1951), 23.

3. Janet Lambert, *Don't Cry, Little Girl* (New York: Grosset & Dunlap, 1952), 141.

4. Thompson, "Rereading Fifties Teen Romance," 373.

5. Thompson, "Rereading Fifties Teen Romance," 382.

6. Thompson, "Rereading Fifties Teen Romance," 382.

7. Society of Phantom Friends, *The Girls' Series Companion* (Rheem Valley, CA: SynSine, 1997), 410.

8. Rosamund Du Jardin, *Double Feature* (New York: J. B. Lippincott Company, 1953), 182.

9. Rosamund Du Jardin, *Double Wedding* (New York: J. B. Lippincott Company, 1959), 99.

10. John M. Murrin, Paul E. Johnson, James M. McPherson, Alice Fahs, and Gary Gerstle, *Liberty, Equality, and Power: A History of the American People* (Belmont, CA: Thomson Wadsworth, 2006), 1032.

11. Du Jardin, *Double Wedding*, 145.

12. Cecile Magaliff, *The Junior Novel: Its Relationship to Adolescent Reading* (Port Washington, NY: Kennikat, 1964), 82.

13. Rosamund Du Jardin, *Showboat Summer* (New York: J. B. Lippincott Company, 1955), 162.

14. Murrin et al., *Liberty, Equality, and Power*, 1034.

15. Rosamund Du Jardin, *Class Ring* (New York: J. B. Lippincott Company, 1951), 137.

16. Du Jardin, *Class Ring*, 138.

17. Magaliff, *The Junior Novel*, 81.

18. Richard S. Alm, "The Glitter and the Gold," *The English Journal*, 44.6 (1955): 318.

19. Anne Emery, *First Love Farewell* (Philadelphia, PA: Westminster, 1958), 169.

20. Emery, *First Love Farewell*, 171.

21. Lucy Rollin, *Twentieth-Century Teen Culture by the Decades* (Westport, CT: Greenwood, 1999), 179–80.

22. Magaliff, *The Junior Novel*, 80.

23. Margaret A. Edwards, "How Do I Love Thee?" *The English Journal*, 41.7 (1952): 336.

24. Margaret A. Edwards, "Let the Lower Lights Be Burning," *The English Journal*, 46.8 (1957), 464.

25. Alm, "The Glitter and the Gold," 315.

26. Edwards, "Let the Lower Lights Be Burning," 465.

27. Bobbie Ann Mason, *The Girl Sleuth* (Athens: University of Georgia Press, 1995), 119–20.

28. Mason, *The Girl Sleuth*, 109.

29. Society of Phantom Friends, *The Girls' Series Companion*, 569.

30. John Axe, *All about Collecting Girls' Series Books* (Grantsville, MD: Hobby House, 2002), 143.

31. Axe, *All about Collecting Girls' Series Books*, 146.

32. "Julie Tatham," in *Something about the Author: Volume 80*, ed. Kevin S. Hile (New York: Gale Research, 1995), 231.

33. Mason, *The Girl Sleuth*, 109.

34. Melanie Rehak, *Girl Sleuth: Nancy Drew and the Women Who Created Her* (Orlando, FL: Harcourt, 2005), 244.

35. Rehak, *Girl Sleuth*, 246.

36. Carole Kismaric and Marvin Heiferman, *The Mysterious Case of Nancy Drew and the Hardy Boys* (New York: Fireside, 1998), 107.

37. Kismaric and Heiferman, *The Mysterious Case of Nancy Drew and the Hardy Boys*, 114.

38. Kismaric and Heiferman, *The Mysterious Case of Nancy Drew and the Hardy Boys*, 114.

39. Margaret Sutton, *The Secret of the Sand Castle* (New York: Grosset & Dunlap, 1967), 5.

40. Society of Phantom Friends, *The Girls' Series Companion*, 241.

41. Kate Emburg, foreword to *Schoolgirl Shamuses, Inc.*, iii.

42. Melanie Knight, *Schoolgirl Shamuses, Inc.* (Rheem Valey, CA: SynSine, 1998), 97.

43. Knight, *Schoolgirl Shamuses, Inc.*, 3.

7

ℰ

Romance Meets Reality: Girls' Series Fiction and the Second Wave of Feminism

While such girls' series books as romances and Nancy Drew mysteries remained popular with teen readers throughout the 1960s, there were few books written for older adolescents. This changed in 1967, however, with the publication of S. E. Hinton's social warfare tale *The Outsiders*.[1] Realistic fiction for teens, focusing on stories about problems in adolescents' lives, became popular in the late 1960s and 1970s. A new literary genre, written specifically for young adult readers, was born. Writers like S. E. Hinton, Paul Zindel, Robert Lipsyte, Alice Childress, and Norma Klein were joined in the 1970s by authors Judy Blume, Richard Peck, Norma Fox Mazer, Harry Mazer, Robert Cormier, and Lois Duncan as the new young adult literati.

One major consequence of this huge change in the landscape of teen publishing involved the cancellation of several popular mystery series aimed at teen readers, including Cherry Ames, Vicki Barr, and Judy Bolton. Teen romances or "junior novels" written by Janet Lambert, Betty Cavanna, Anne Emery, and Rosamund Du Jardin became dated as adolescents became more sexually active, a change encouraged by the availability of the birth control pill. By the end of the 1960s, many popular series and authors of light, innocent teen stories had virtually disappeared, replaced by authors who explored social problems experienced by contemporary teens. It is disturbing to note that career women Cherry Ames, Vicki Barr, and Penny Parrish became obsolete during a decade that championed women's rights. But it was their traditionally female roles as nurse, airline stewardess, and actress that were outdated. Instead, the women's liberation movement sought to gain women the right to pursue the same professional careers as men, along with equal pay for women in the workplace, and such jobs as nurse and airline stewardess were the kind of female jobs many women wanted to leave behind by the late 1960s.

Amateur detectives, including Nancy Drew, The Dana Girls, Trixie Belden, and Judy Bolton, remained popular throughout the 1960s. While the Stratemeyer Syndicate and the Western Publishing Company worked hard to keep their girl detectives current with fashion and technology, author Margaret Sutton failed to update Judy Bolton, and publisher Grosset & Dunlap cancelled the series in 1967.

Mystery series produced by the Stratemeyer Syndicate, like Nancy Drew and The Dana Girls, remained popular. In fact, the women's liberation movement raised Nancy Drew to new heights of popularity, despite revisions to Nancy's character that made her less legendary and more ordinary. Although Nancy never claimed to be part of the second wave of feminism, younger teen readers claimed her as their icon, likely encouraged by mothers who remembered a bolder and more assertive Nancy Drew. A television show featuring Nancy helped her gain even more fame. In the 1970s, Nancy Drew became a symbol for the intelligent, independent, and adventurous young women that readers dreamed of becoming, even though they knew Nancy lived in a fantasy world.

Teen Romance, Career, and Mystery Series

During the 1960s, teen romance stories were still available, although they were less popular than during the 1950s. Janet Lambert continued her Parrish Family series, which focused on Penny and her sister Tippy during the 1940s and 1950s. Written in 1962, *Introducing Parri* introduces readers to Penny's fourteen-year-old daughter, Parri MacDonald, and her cousin, Davy Parrish. Parri is lonely and unhappy at boarding school, so she rebels by traveling to New York, where she buys expensive clothing and auditions for a Broadway play. Her parents, Penny and Josh, realize that their busy careers as actress and producer don't leave them much time for their shy daughter.

Penny Parrish, who juggled career and family during the 1950s, is portrayed during the 1960s as a career woman who doesn't have enough time for her daughter. In *Stagestruck Parri* and *My Davy*, Parri tries to convince her parents that she's ready to become an actress, like her mother. But Parri, who is sixteen when she asks for an agent in *My Davy*, discovers that her parents think she's too young to become a professional actress. Davy Parrish, a polio victim, struggles to pass his West Point Academy physical and to fit in at school. The stories show a strong relationship between cousins Parri and Davy, and rather than romance, the books focus on their career aspirations and plans. The Parrish family stories ended in 1969, with *Here's Marny*, featuring Tippy and Peter Jordan and their foster daughter, Marny.

In 1959, Anne Emery launched Dinny Gordon, a series about a teen girl who is more interested in her future career as an archaeologist than boys and dating. She dates a few male friends so she can attend dances and parties, but she doesn't want to get involved in a serious relationship. She has many friends of both sexes, and she is portrayed as "bright, amusing, independent, empathetic, and tolerant."[2]

Through the early 1960s, Dinny grew up. She finally falls for Curt Beauregard in *Dinny Gordon, Sophomore*, but he is dating her friend Sue, so she waits until he is free to date again. Eventually Curt wants to go steady, but Dinny is not sure that she wants to date only one boy. She says of the dating game, "It's like walking into a trap."[3] The relationship is in trouble when Dinny and Curt argue about his anti-Semitic attitudes. Dinny likes Debby and Mike Goldman, and she doesn't understand why some of her friends, including Curt, are prejudiced against them. Dinny breaks up with Curt at the end of *Dinny Gordon, Junior*.

In the final book in the series, Dinny dates Steve Dennison and nearly allows the needy boy to derail her future plans, including her summer trip to Europe and the Middle East after graduation. Dinny eventually gets tired of typing Steve's term papers and dumps him. She goes to the prom with her friend Tom and, at the end of the story, she leaves on her trip confident that college man Brad Kenyon will be waiting for her at her university. Readers know that Dinny won't let a man interfere with her career goals again. In Emery's Pat Marlowe series, published in the late 1950s, Pat finally realizes that she would rather pursue an acting career than a boy who doesn't share her interest in the theater. Since many of the 1950s romances suggest that girls should go steady with a boy, go to college, get married, and become homemakers, Emery's Pat Marlowe and Dinny Gordon series are refreshing for their messages that women should experience both fulfilling relationships and careers.

Although Emery doesn't touch such controversial political issues as the birth control pill, which was approved by the Federal Drug Administration in 1960, her Dinny Gordon series signals a change in women's roles in society. Librarian Joyce Litton argues: "[Dinny's] attitude foreshadows what would become a common trend of women delaying marriage and a family until they are established in their careers. Emery was a path breaker in presenting this idea to adolescent readers."[4] Betty Friedan wrote about the bored suburban housewife who suffered from "the problem that has no name" in her book *The Feminine Mystique* in 1963, beginning a women's liberation movement in the United States.[5]

In 1966, the year after the last book in the Dinny Gordon series was published, the National Organization for Women was founded by Friedan and other prominent women's and civil rights activists. Through the second half of the decade, the National Organization for Women supported an Equal Rights Amendment (ERA) to the Constitution that would give women the same legal rights as men, but the ERA became controversial in the early 1970s, when conservative women's groups successfully protested the amendment, arguing against such a radical change.

As a result of many women's desires to inhabit both the public and private spheres of American society, romantic stories for teen girls met reality during the 1960s, and the publishing industry shifted focus away from romance and family life in teen fiction. While the new young adult literature dealt with such serious issues as sex, providing a bleak picture of options available to pregnant teens in Ann Head's *Mr. and Mrs. Bo Jo Jones* and Paul Zindel's *My Darling, My Hamburger*, girls' series fiction continued to ignore sex and its consequences. Although girls' series authors ignored the sexual revolution, some clearly supported the women's liberation movement. As we have seen, Emery's Dinny Gordon and Pat Marlowe series suggest that young women should put education and careers ahead of romance, marriage, and family. Joyce Litton argues,

> Emery is a transitional author whose work provides a bridge between the 1950s presentation of family life as portrayed in the television series *Ozzie and Harriet* and the mid- to late-1960s career-oriented lifestyle advocated by Betty Friedan, Gloria Steinem, and other leaders of the newly developing women's movement.[6]

But the idea of women combining careers and family was not entirely new to girls' series fiction. Janet Lambert had already introduced readers to a career woman in the late 1940s. Although Penny Parrish continued to be a role model for women who wanted both careers and families, Lambert never told her young readers that it was easy to do it all, and readers experienced Penny's challenges as actress, wife, and mother, juggling everything right along with her.

Girls' series featuring young career women, created to entice teens into working during World War II, had morphed into mystery series during the 1950s. Advertising executive Connie Blair, whose author abandoned the series in the late 1950s, was revived twice in the 1960s by publisher Grosset & Dunlap, once in hardcover and once in paperback. Her final appearance during the 1970s was in paperback.

In the early 1960s, author Helen Wells continued to write about airline stewardess Vicki Barr's adventures. When Vicki gets a new job at Worldwide Airlines in *The Clue of the Carved Ruby*, she even has the chance to travel outside the United States. Vicki keeps busy tracking a missing heiress across the United States, searching for stolen jewels in France, getting hijacked and held hostage on a tropical island in South America, and thwarting thieves in India. Published in 1964, *The Brass Idol Mystery* was Vicki Barr's last adventure. Girls' series book collector John Axe laments the fact that Vicki Barr became outdated:

> It is a shame that Vicki's career was not transferred from flight attendant to pilot, as it would have given Helen Wells the possibility of developing a more contemporary series heroine. Vicki Barr could have been one with whom young women of the 1970s and beyond would have identified.[7]

By 1968, Helen Wells's other career girl, Cherry Ames, was also out of work. Nurse Cherry Ames spent some of the 1960s working in such traditional settings as hospitals and doctor's offices. In *The Mystery in the Doctor's Office*, Cherry even has a little romance with Dr. Grey Russell. More worrying than the appearance of romance, however, is that Cherry sometimes seems too unsure of herself for a career woman with her experience. Cherry Ames no longer resembles the independent and assertive young woman readers first met during World War II. Of course, to make Cherry seem like a young nurse, her years of experience and Army service during World War II are absent in these later books.

In the 1960s, Cherry finally gets the opportunity to visit exciting locations again. She travels to Canada, England, Kenya, and Switzerland on nursing assignments. In *Cherry Ames, Jungle Nurse*, Cherry helps establish a health clinic in Kenya and breaks up a smuggling ring at the same time. In the last title in the series, published in 1968, Cherry stumbles onto a mystery at a Swiss ski resort in *Ski Nurse Mystery*.

Vicki Barr and Cherry Ames author Helen Wells was unhappy when her girls' series were cancelled, so she decided to do something about it. In 1970, Wells reportedly chaired a Publishing Practices Committee of the Board of the Mystery Writers of America, which sought to investigate the alleged shabby treatment of series authors by the Stratemeyer Syndicate and publisher Grosset & Dunlap. Series authors suspected that Grosset & Dunlap was working in cahoots with the Stratemeyer Syndicate to put all girls' series books, with the exception of those published by the Stratemeyer Syndicate, out of print for good.

In a letter to Judy Bolton author Margaret Sutton, Wells stated, "My semiannual G & D royalties for 1969, for U.S. and foreign, was about [$]1600. Or was it less? I am so disgusted I forget the exact figure."[8] The Society of Phantom Friends reports that nothing ever happened with the Publishing Practices Committee, despite Wells's efforts to collect information from authors about the marketing of their books and royalties, because authors decided not to follow through with any action. The Mystery Writers of America, moreover, claims no knowledge of the Publishing Practices Committee chaired by Helen Wells.[9]

Nevertheless, the Cherry Ames series reappeared twice in the 1970s. Four books were reissued in paperback under new titles in 1972, and three of these were reissued again in 1978. Perhaps Helen Wells gave up the fight for her series due to lack of support from other authors, or perhaps she was placated when Cherry Ames came back into print. It is unlikely, however, that Wells made very much money from the reissue of a handful of books from one of her popular series.

During the 1960s, such amateur girl detectives as Judy Bolton and Trixie Belden continued to be popular with readers. Trixie Belden and her friends travel across the United States, solving mysteries in Iowa, New York City, St. Louis, and Mississippi. Trixie and the Bob-Whites of the Glen find evil everywhere they go. True to the girl detective form, Trixie searches for hidden treasure and missing jewels, receives strange prophecies, and finds mysteries in old letters. Through it all, fourteen-year-old Trixie has so much fun, she is determined to run her own detective agency when she grows up.

Judy Bolton continued to solve mysteries as an amateur detective until 1967. Judy travels across the United States solving mysteries in exciting places like New York and Washington, D.C. In *The Whispered Watchword*, Judy, Peter, and Blackberry the cat solve the mystery of a whispering statue in the Capitol Rotunda in Washington, D.C. Although Margaret Sutton didn't know her series was going to be cancelled when she wrote *The Puzzle in the Pond*, it comes full circle when Judy travels back to her hometown of Roulsville to find furniture belonging to her family. While thirty-one years have passed in real time, it is only six years since the flood destroyed Roulsville in Judy Bolton's world. Both Sutton and Judy Bolton were becoming outdated after more than thirty years in the publishing business.

In *The Secret of the Sand Castle*, the last book in the series published in 1967, Judy goes to Fire Island to help her cousin Roxie claim her inheritance. Although Judy Bolton fans report another book in the series titled *The Strange Likeness*, Sutton never completed it because the series was cancelled by Grosset & Dunlap. Sutton was bitterly disappointed when her beloved series was cancelled and, like Helen Wells, she blamed the Stratemeyer Syndicate and publisher Grosset & Dunlap. In a letter to Wells in 1970, Sutton complained about the lack of marketing for her series:

> I am sure you know that for years I have been aware of the strangle hold the Stratemeyer Syndicate has over Grosset and Dunlap. I should have

objected as far back as 1950 when my sales began to drop because the Stratemeyer Syndicate insisted on cutting out the advertising that used to appear on the backs of the Nancy Drew series. . . . I could see then that series books were gradually becoming a Stratemeyer monopoly. . . . It is now impossible to obtain Judy's in the stores.[10]

Sutton reported that her royalties for 1969 were less than $1,000.[11] In 1967 and 1968, Grosset & Dunlap reissued revised versions of the first four Judy Bolton books in paperback, likely accounting for any royalties Sutton received in 1969.

Although the sexual revolution and feminist movement were absent from girls' series books, by the early 1970s both had impacted women's lives and popular culture in the United States. Television shows featuring independent working women, for instance, *That Girl* and *Mary Tyler Moore*, struck a chord with young women. *Ms. Magazine*, covering such feminist issues as the ERA, abortion, sexual harassment, and domestic violence, was launched in 1971. Although the ERA failed to pass in Congress in 1973, feminists were ecstatic when the Supreme Court ruled in *Roe v. Wade* that antiabortion laws violated women's privacy rights. Although the ERA had failed, the women's liberation movement brought women new reproductive rights.

While Judy Blume treated issues of sex, birth control, pregnancy, and abortion from the perspectives of liberated young women in her 1975 novel *Forever*, girls' series books still avoided these issues by keeping romance very light. Surprisingly, girls' series featuring career women were phased out by publishers during the early years of the second wave of feminism. By the 1970s, career women were scarce in new girls' series books, and they could only be found in a few reissues and older series still carried by libraries.

The Stratemeyer Syndicate Girl Detectives

Girl detectives were still popular in the 1960s and 1970s, and the Stratemeyer Syndicate continued to publish their popular mysteries series, including Nancy Drew and The Dana Girls. The Stratemeyer Syndicate also introduced a new girls' mystery series, Linda Craig, which featured horses. The horse theme captured few fans, and Linda Craig was cancelled after six books in 1964. Several titles in the Kay Tracey series were reissued, once in the 1960s and once in the 1970s, with updated cover art. Along with new titles in the series, the revisions to the original books in the Nancy Drew series continued to remove racist portrayals and update fashions and technologies. Harriet Adams, who ran the Stratemeyer Syndicate, took the opportunity to make changes to Nancy Drew's character. "Nancy, as I knew her, was on the verge of disappearing forever from print," former Nancy Drew ghostwriter Mildred Wirt observed.[12]

While Adams and her employees worked hard to update the original books in the Nancy Drew series, Nancy, Bess, and George found exciting new adventures, traveling the world and solving mysteries in Hong Kong, Scotland, Peru, Paris, Africa, Turkey, and Tokyo. The Dana Girls continued to solve mysteries at home and at Starhurst boarding school through the 1960s. By the 1970s, however, The Dana Girls series was revised, dropping some titles and adding new ones.

Although cover art for the Nancy Drew and The Dana Girls books display the teen protagonists in contemporary clothing and hairstyles, and the dialogue contains modern slang, Adams refused to let her girls become hippies. As Adams told a reporter from the *New York Times* about the Stratemeyer Syndicate's series, "They don't have hippies in them. . . . And none of the characters have love affairs or get pregnant or take dope. If they did, I'm sure that would be the end of the series."[13] Nancy Drew and The Dana Girls, who probably would have enjoyed some of the freedoms espoused by hippies and feminists, missed out on the protests, the consciousness-raising groups, and the sexual revolution.

It is ironic that during the women's liberation movement, Nancy Drew was becoming a more ordinary teenage girl. But young readers were not familiar with the assertive, bold, and independent Nancy designed by ghostwriter Wirt, and they enjoyed reading about the adventures of the toned-down, smart, and modest girl detective recreated by Adams. In an interview with a reporter from the *Philadelphia Bulletin Sunday Magazine*, Adams stated, "I wasn't thinking about women's liberation when I wrote the books. . . . I've never thought of myself as a women's libber, but I do believe that women have brains. Nothing makes me angrier than to have my intelligence insulted."[14] Adams, who was in her late seventies, accidentally created a new Nancy that girls growing up during the second wave of feminism could admire. Adams was very protective of the Nancy Drew she was recreating during this time. "Woe to any Grosset and Dunlap executive, editor, or illustrator who crossed Harriet's path or tried to dilute her new vision of Nancy Drew," declare Stratemeyer Syndicate historians Carole Kismaric and Marvin Heiferman.[15]

Readers responded by buying Nancy Drew books in record numbers. Sales of the books, which had lagged during the 1950s, began to go up again. By 1969, Nancy Drew had sold more than thirty million books, and the series continued to sell more than a million copies a year.[16] Between 1972 and 1977, sales of Nancy Drew books broke records at Grosset & Dunlap, earning the publisher and the Stratemeyer Syndicate more money than ever. In 1974, Adams's sister Edna died, leaving her share of the Stratemeyer Syndicate to her sister. Another business partner, Andy Svenson, died the next year, and Adams bought his share of the company from his widow. By the mid-1970s, Adams had complete control of the Stratemeyer Syndicate, and she worked with several assistants to carry on writing their popular series, including The Dana Girls, The Hardy Boys, The Bobbsey Twins, and Nancy Drew.

When the women's liberation movement brought such strong, smart female characters as *Mary Tyler Moore*, *Wonder Woman*, and *The Bionic Woman* to television in the 1970s, it was only natural that Nancy Drew should join them. In 1977, ABC launched *The Hardy Boys/Nancy Drew Mysteries*, starring Pamela Sue Martin as beloved girl detective Nancy Drew. While teen idols Shaun Cassidy and Parker Stevenson were a hit as The Hardy Boys, fans failed to respond to Pamela Sue Martin's portrayal of Nancy, and she left the show after the first season. Fans also hated the melding of Nancy's best friends, Bess Marvin and George Fayne, into one character, who was named George, but had long blonde hair and behaved like shy, giggly Bess. Actress Janet Louise Johnson replaced Pamela Sue Martin the following year, when the show merged completely with *The Hardy Boys*. Tomboy George's hair was cut short, and a character named Bess Marvin was added.

But ultimately, Harriet Adams's insistence that the show avoid sex, drugs, and violence made the series too wholesome and boring for prime-time television. *Nancy Drew* was phased out in 1978, and *The Hardy Boys* was cancelled in 1979. While a wholesome Nancy Drew was popular with her younger readers, Nancy didn't have enough sex appeal for a wider television audience, and she was no competition for the sexy young women detectives on *Charlie's Angels*. Pamela Sue Martin, who didn't want her career to be hindered by the wholesome Nancy Drew image, posed as a sexy version of the teen sleuth for the popular men's magazine *Playboy*. Adams was reportedly "fit to be tied."[17]

Although women's liberation didn't help Nancy Drew become popular on television, it did change the way business was done at the Stratemeyer Syndicate. Ironically, Harriet Adams believed she, like other women writers of girls' series books, was being poorly treated by publisher Grosset & Dunlap. Although authors Helen Wells and Margaret Sutton thought there was a conspiracy between the Stratemeyer Syndicate and Grosset & Dunlap to put their series out of publication, they were unaware of Adams's struggles since the early 1950s to meet the publisher's demands for revisions, new titles, and strict deadlines.

Moreover, Adams had never been able to get Grosset & Dunlap to agree to the new, graduated royalty rates commonly paid in publishing. Instead, the Stratemeyer Syndicate was still being paid 4 percent royalties, according to a deal negotiated by her father decades earlier.[18] But Adams was loyal to her long-time publisher, and she was reluctant to confront problems in their business dealings.

In the late 1970s, Adams made her assistants junior partners in the Stratemeyer Syndicate, and these younger partners convinced her to try negotiating again with Grosset & Dunlap. When Grosset & Dunlap refused to renegotiate, Adams and her partners found a new publisher in Simon & Schuster. They sold the rights to all new books produced by the Stratemeyer Syndicate, including titles in the Nancy Drew, Hardy Boys, and Bobbsey Twins series, to Simon & Schuster in 1979. The Dana Girls got lost in the shuffle and virtually disappeared, although books in the series remained on library shelves throughout the next decade.

Simon & Schuster issued new Nancy Drew titles in paperback, beginning with *The Triple Hoax*, in late 1979. When publishers Grosset & Dunlap realized they were about to lose their most lucrative girls' series, they filed a lawsuit against the Stratemeyer Syndicate "for breach of contract and copyright infringement, eventually asking for

$300 million in damages."[19] While Grosset & Dunlap was preparing for a lawsuit, Simon & Schuster was getting ready to celebrate the fiftieth anniversary of their famous girl sleuth in style.

Although career and romance girls' series faded away during the late 1960s with the advent of the new young adult literature genre, mystery series were still going strong, especially Nancy Drew. By the mid-1970s, Nancy Drew became a feminist icon for young women who grew up during the second wave of feminism in the United States. A backlash against the independent girl sleuth was gearing up in the late 1970s, however, when publishers like Scholastic Book Services and Bantam Books prepared to bring back teen romance series. But no one, least of all the publishers, expected the huge explosion of teen romance series that would dominate young adult publishing during the next decade.

Notes

1. Michael Cart, *From Romance to Realism: 50 Years of Growth and Change in Young Adult Literature* (New York: HarperCollins, 1996), 43–44.

2. Joyce Litton, "Dinny Gordon: Proto-Feminist," *The Journal of American Culture*, 29.1 (2006): 44.

3. Anne Emery, *Dinny Gordon, Sophomore* (Philadelphia: Macrae Smith Company, 1961), 172.

4. Litton, "Dinny Gordon," 47.

5. Betty Friedan, *The Feminine Mystique* (New York: W. W. Norton & Company, 1963), 15.

6. Litton, "Dinny Gordon," 43.

7. John Axe, *All about Collecting Girls' Series Books* (Grantsville, MD: Hobby House, 2002), 143.

8. Society of Phantom Friends, *A Guide to Judy Bolton Country* (Rheem Valley, CA: SynSine, 2004), 71.

9. Society of Phantom Friends, *A Guide to Judy Bolton Country*, 74.

10. Society of Phantom Friends, *A Guide to Judy Bolton Country*, 73.

11. Society of Phantom Friends, *A Guide to Judy Bolton Country*, 73.

12. Mildred Wirt Benson, "The Nancy I Knew," introduction to *The Mystery at Lilac Inn*, by Carolyn Keene (1931; reprint, Bedford, MA: Applewood Books, 1994), vii.

13. Judy Klemesrud, "100 Books—and Not a Hippie in Them," *The New York Times* (April 4, 1968): 52.

14. Rose Dewolf, "The *Real* Mystery behind Nancy Drew," *Philadelphia Bulletin Sunday Magazine* (January 13, 1974): 4.

15. Carole Kismaric and Marvin Heiferman, *The Mysterious Case of Nancy Drew and the Hardy Boys* (New York: Fireside, 1998), 114.

16. Melanie Rehak, *Girl Sleuth: Nancy Drew and the Women Who Created Her* (Orlando, FL: Harcourt, 2005), 264, 270.

17. Rehak, *Girl Sleuth*, 286.

18. Rehak, *Girl Sleuth*, 289.

19. Rehak, *Girl Sleuth*, 290.

8

Sweet Dreams for Teen Queens: Romance Renaissance in the Reagan Era

Such teen romance series as Wildfire, Sweet Dreams, and Sweet Valley High were popular with preteen and teen readers during the 1980s. Book critic Selma Lanes argued that as early as 1981, "The commercial success of preteen and teenage romance series is the publishing phenomenon of the decade."[1] Later in the decade, young adult literature expert Patty Campbell agreed, "Easily the most significant development in books for teens in the past ten years has been the rise of the formula paperback series like Sweet Valley High and the consequent recognition of the potential of the YA market by trade paperback publishers and booksellers."[2] Francine Pascal, creator of the tremendously popular Sweet Valley High soap opera series, was the queen of teen series fiction.

Several trends in American society set the stage for the publishing and popularity of teen romance novels, including the conservative society, created with the election of President Ronald Reagan, the emergence of a powerful New Right movement, and the publishing of original novels in paperback. Feminist scholar Linda Christian-Smith argues, "Although I do not believe that there is an outright conspiracy between teen romance publishers and the New Right . . . it is the case that more and more segments of the culture industry, particularly publishing, are owned by large corporations whose interests are politically conservative."[3]

During the 1980s, publishers started printing more original stories in paperback, especially in such genres as romance and science fiction, rather than simply reprinting best-selling hardcover novels in paperback. "Paperback books gained a newfound respectability in the 1980s as consumers tired of paying the rising cost of hardbacks."[4] This change enabled publishers to create and market paperback books for young adults. Publishers and book packagers created original paperback romance series, modeled after adult romance series only with more innocent storylines, for teen readers. Generation X teens had "a staggering $45 billion" a year to spend, and girls could buy these new paperback books with their allowances and babysitting money while shopping with friends at the mall.[5] Young adult literature critic Michael Cart argues that the romance phenomenon was significant "because it signaled the emergence of a new marketplace—the chain bookstore—and the emergence of a new type of book: the paperback original."[6]

Contemporary Teen Romance Series

Contemporary teen romance series, like Wildfire, Sweet Dreams, and First Love from Silhouette, featured single titles written by different authors under a series name and logo. The books were usually between 40,000 to 50,000 words, making them short and easy reads. Wendy Smith describes the contemporary romance series:

> The heroine is 15–17, the boy slightly older. The story is told from the girl's point of view. The action takes place in a suburb or small town. There is no explicit sex or profanity. Although romance is the focus, the story may also deal with other adolescent problems. The ending is upbeat. Readership is assumed to be girls aged 12–16.[7]

This description of the novels is a bit simplistic. Because the story is told from the girl's perspective, her character is usually more fully developed than that of the boy involved in the romantic story. The male characters often seem a bit flat, but that was not important, because the books actually focused on the development and growth of the female protagonist in romance and other areas of her life. It is useful to examine the most popular series individually, since each series tried to differentiate itself from the others.

Love Comes to Anne, the first title in Scholastic Book Services Wildfire series, started a teen paperback romance boom. The series literally sold like wildfire, selling 1.8 million copies of sixteen titles in the first year.[8] "Every Young Girl's Dream of Love" was the slogan used to sell these new teen romances. When editors at Scholastic noticed that romantic stories were selling well through their school book clubs in the late 1970s, they created the Wildfire romance series and marketed it directly to teen readers. This was revolutionary. Young adult books were typically sold to libraries or parents, and it was the responsibility of librarians and parents to encourage young adults to read the books. Scholastic began advertising the series directly to teen readers through their school book clubs, their books, magazine ads, and a new *Wildfire* magazine. An advertisement at the back of *A Kiss for Tomorrow* by Maud Johnson proclaimed, "Did you like this Wildfire romance? Then you'll love all the other Wildfire girls. They're a little bit of *you!*"[9]

The protagonist is usually sixteen years old. While she may have dated boys before, she has never been in love. Sometimes the boy she falls in love with is a little older, which adds complications to the love story. In Lucille Warner's *Love Comes to Anne*, Pierre wants to marry Anne and live with her on his family's vineyard in France. Although Anne's parents object, the decision is Anne's to make. She decides she wants to go to college before she gets married. In Terry Morris's *Just Sixteen*, Nancy is worried that Roger will forget about her when he goes to college. Although the girls consider such serious issues as marriage or going away to school with a boyfriend, affections do not progress beyond kissing, hugging, and holding hands. Despite the series name, Wildfire girls are neither wild, nor full of passion and fire. Instead, they are caught up in the emotions of first love and first kisses.

Like adult romance novels, Wildfire romances focus on the emotions of the female protagonist as she experiences her first love, but the female protagonists are often busy with their friends and extracurricular activities, too. Sometimes the girls have other ordinary teenage problems that create obstacles to romance. For instance, family and friends often praise Angel Porter for her beauty in Helen Cavanagh's *Angel*, but she wants to be loved for her strong character and carpentry talents rather than her looks. Sometimes girls in Wildfire romances get too caught up in their first romance, and it is up to their friends to help them see that there is more to life than romance. In Jane Claypool Miner's *Senior Class*, shy Mary Murray finally has a boyfriend. Mary thinks about joining her boyfriend, Whit, at his university, but neither her Aunt Sarah nor her friend Sandy believes Mary is ready for such a serious relationship. Sandy helps bring Mary back to reality:

> "Seems to me that before you can even think about getting a man, you'd better think about exactly who you are. You know, life can be very tough on women who can't take care of themselves. You should look at the statistics on divorce before you just lie down and let some man take care of you." Sandy paused and took a deep break before she added, "Besides which, if you don't have any interests or skills of your own, what man is going to want you anyhow?"[10]

Although the Wildfire series was popular with teens, some parents did not appreciate it. Elaine Wagner was horrified by the contents of her daughter's *Wildfire* magazine: "A collection of girl's romances and how-to-snag-a-boy advice, it was the most sexist material I had seen in years."[11] Wagner launched a successful protest campaign, forcing Scholastic to cancel the magazine. She also participated in a task force to help Scholastic staff understand the lack of sex and race equity in the series. Perhaps Jane Claypool Miner's *Senior Class* is a result of Wagner's work with the publisher. The Wildfire romance series continued to publish, reaching a total of approximately eighty books by 1986, when it was cancelled.

Several other publishers decided to take advantage of Wildfire's success in 1981, launching such new paperback romance lines as Bantam's Sweet Dreams and Harlequin's First Love from Silhouette, with "whopping first runs" of 150,000 and 190,000, respectively.[12] Grosset & Dunlap published the contemporary Caprice romance series; Dell began promoting backlist titles under the Young Love brand; and Scholastic continued to add new romance lines, including the serious Wishing Star series in 1981, the contemporary gothic Windswept series in 1982, and the historical Sunfire series in 1984.

In 1980, Bantam Books asked book packager Cloverdale Press, owned by brothers Jeffrey and Daniel Weiss, to produce a line of teen romances. *Publisher's Weekly* reported, "The Weiss's responded with the name Sweet Dreams, invited some of the country's prettiest teen models for shootings, solicited manuscripts from agents, and nine months later, handed in the first six Sweet Dreams titles."[13] To launch the Sweet Dreams romances in September 1981, Bantam Books and Cloverdale Press chose a story with a very unhappy ending in Barbara Conklin's *P.S. I Love You*. In the story, aspiring romance writer Mariah meets Paul Strobe when her single mother takes a housesitting job in Palm Springs for the summer. Only after they fall in love does Paul tell her he has leukemia. Mariah's summer love ends sadly when Paul dies, but Mariah writes about the experience of her first love, creating her first romance novel. More memorable than most of the 233 titles in the series because of the unhappy ending, *P.S. I Love You* began a fourteen-year run for the Sweet Dreams series, making it the longest running single title teen romance series of the 1980s.

For the most part, the Sweet Dreams series was lighter than Wildfire romances, with less emphasis on the confusing emotions of first loves. The female protagonist usually thinks she's lost the boy of her dreams, only to find out that he really loves her. For instance, in Rosemary Vernon's *The Popularity Plan*, Frannie Bronson's transformation from shy to popular is so dramatic that she nearly loses Ronnie, the talented artist she truly loves. In Gailanne Maravel's *Lights, Camera, Love*, soap opera star Holly Giles alienates her new boyfriend, Tim, when she behaves like her television character so she can become friends with popular girls at her new private school.

The Sweet Dreams series lasted until 1995, several years longer than its competitors, because the stories were light, innocent love stories that were quick and easy to read. In 1995, Bantam phased out Sweet Dreams and created a new, similar series called Love Stories. The difference, according to an ad in the final Sweet Dreams books, was that Love Stories would include boys' perspectives on love relationships.

Billed as "America's Favorite Teenage Romance," First Love from Silhouette was created by romance publisher Harlequin. The series was launched in October 1981, one month after Sweet Dreams came on the market. Silhouette created a $1.4 million advertising campaign that included ads for teen magazines, radio, and television. According to *Publishers Weekly* magazine, "Common adolescent problems and traumas—a new boy in school, wanting to be a cheerleader or star of the school play, going out on a first date—are the dramas behind First Loves."[14]

For instance, in Elaine Harper's *Short Stop for Romance*, Celia realizes that she loves her softball coach, Mark, but she thinks their relationship is just business for him. In Bea Alexander's *Advice and Consent*, Lori is confused by her new feelings for old friend Ian Winslow. The protagonist of Cheryl Zach's *Waiting for Amanda* must deal with heavier issues than some girls her age. Amanda becomes responsible for her little sister and aging aunt when her mother dies, and she refuses to accept help, even from handsome Ty Kendall. Later books in the First Love series include mystery and suspense stories. In 1987, after publishing 236 titles, the series was replaced with the Crosswinds series and Keepsakes series, which only lasted for about a year. The Crosswinds series published R. L. Stine's first horror novel for teens, *Blind Date*, beginning Stine's career as a popular author of horror fiction for children and teens.

Cover art was a very important factor in the sales and popularity of teen romance novels. Some contemporary romance series, like First Love from Silhouette, featured teen couples on the covers, while other series, like Sweet Dreams, usually featured teen girls alone. This is ironic since the stories were billed as romance stories. The cover art usually featured beautiful teenagers who were actually models, so the teens on the covers didn't necessarily look like real people; they looked like models. But publishers were aware that the covers had to attract the attention of teenage girls, so they used models to sell the books. Ron Beuhl, editorial director at Bantam, explains, "We're selling jeans on the outside and happy family stories on the inside, but you have to sell the books the way the jeans are sold."[15] Indeed, the cover of Yvonne Greene's Sweet Dreams title *Cover Girl* features a picture of a girl modeling Jordache jeans. Models selected for the covers of the romance novels were often recognizable faces from such teen magazines as *Seventeen* and *Teen*. For instance, the Sweet Dreams title *The Two of Us*, by Janet Quin-Harkin, features Academy Award-winning actress Jennifer Connelly, who began her career as a child actress and teen model. Another Quin-Harkin title, *Follow That Boy*, features Lisa

Whelchel, who played spoiled rich girl Blair Warner on the popular 1980s television show *Facts of Life*. Cover art also alluded to popular music and music videos. In Shannon Blair's *Star Struck!* Carrie wins the part as an extra in a Michael Jackson music video, and the cover shows a Michael Jackson impersonator posing with the young model, wearing Jackson's signature red leather jacket from the popular *Thriller* video.

Whether the books featured teen couples or teenage girls on their covers, it was clear that the books were targeted at teenage girls. Readers were attracted to the books by their covers and the promise of an innocent story of first love.

Soap Opera Teen Romance Series

In 1983, Bantam introduced the first soap-opera romance series, Sweet Valley High. Such television soap operas as *General Hospital* and *Another World* were becoming more popular with teens, and soap operas were introducing more teen characters to attract young adult viewers. Author Francine Pascal wanted to write a soap opera for television similar to *Dallas*, a popular prime-time soap opera, aimed at young adults. Instead, an editor suggested that she write a soap opera in series book form. "Each book, I concluded, would have to be a complete story in itself," Pascal once explained, "but with a hook ending to lead you to the sequel. The series would have to have vivid continuing characters. When I came up with the idea for Elizabeth and Jessica, the Jeckyll and Hyde twins, I was off and running."[16] Pascal wrote a thirty-page Sweet Valley Bible that ghostwriters, like author Eileen Goudge, used to write the books in the series. Pascal outlined each book, and the ghostwriters filled in the details. Ghostwriters were hired by Cloverdale Press, a book packaging firm that also produced the Sweet Dreams romance series, who worked with Pascal to produce the books.[17]

Sweet Valley High featured sixteen-year-old identical twins Elizabeth and Jessica Wakefield, who closely resembled Rosamund Du Jardin's fictional 1950s twins Pam and Penny Howard. Elizabeth is the good, studious twin who wants to be a journalist, while self-centered Jessica only thinks about boys, clothes, and having a good time. Jessica is a typical California valley girl, without the 1980s slang. Pascal explains, "The trick is to think of Elizabeth and Jessica as the good and bad sides of one person."[18] In the first book in the series, *Double Love*, Jessica and Elizabeth vie for the attentions of Todd Wilkins, a handsome basketball player. Jessica only wants Todd's attention because he seems to like Elizabeth more than her, and eventually good wins over evil when Elizabeth and Todd declare their love for each other and share a kiss goodnight. The plot is very similar to Du Jardin's *Double Date*.

The Wakefield twins' friends and family, including their parents and brother, Steven, round out the cast of characters in the series. Adults played a fairly minor role. The stories usually focused on the twins, but secondary characters were also featured. Elizabeth spends her spare time with boyfriend Todd Wilkins and best friend Enid Rollins, while Jessica spends much of her time shopping and hanging out with her wealthy best friend, Lila Fowler, and the girls from her cheerleading squad. Elizabeth often bails Jessica out of trouble, sometimes by impersonating her twin.

In the early books in the series, the Wakefield twins and their friends deal with light issues teens confront on a daily basis, for instance arguments with friends and siblings, crushes on boys, the desire to become a cheerleader, peer pressure, rivalry, and popularity. The series occasionally deals with more serious matters, like illness, death, and divorce. All the issues addressed in the series, however, are handled in dramatic soap opera fashion, whether the problems are large or small.

Pascal argues, "I made Sweet Valley a place right out of MGM. Total fantasy . . . I didn't intend Sweet Valley to be realistic. . . . It is a soap opera in book form."[19] However, when fans of the series began writing letters to Pascal saying how real the books were for them, Pascal decided to make the stories more realistic, adding minority characters. The stories, nevertheless, still seemed like fantasies to some young readers. There was never any doubt, however, about the popularity of the series. "In 1985, the first young adult novel ever to reach the *New York Times* paperback bestseller list was a Sweet Valley High Super Edition . . . called *Perfect Summer*," reports librarian Mary M. Huntwork.[20]

Over time, the series changed to include elements of other genres, including the Super Thriller editions featuring mystery and suspense; Super Stars editions telling stories of secondary characters; and Magna editions, featuring books about a third evil twin, Elizabeth and Jessica's secret diaries, and stories focusing on the history of Sweet Valley's prominent families.

With the popularity of the Sweet Valley High series, such new soap opera series as Cheerleaders, Seniors, and Girls of Canby Hall were soon popular. Christian romances aimed at teens, including Christy Miller, Sierra Jensen, and Cedar River Daydreams, were also available. In the Christian romances, the primary love interest is God, and the secondary love interest is the boy, adding complicated issues to the romance. These romance series were popular because teens struggle with the same issues in real life, and Christian romances give teens a chance to learn how fictional Christian teens deal with religion, love, and relationships.

No other soap opera series, however, was able to match the success of Sweet Valley High. There were two secrets to its popularity. First, the series began to incorporate more sexual activity into the stories. Soap opera romance series like Sweet Valley High kept pace with changing attitudes about sexuality in American society, while such romance series as Wildfire and First Love from Silhouette did not. These series became outdated, and young adults were no longer interested in reading them. Wildfire and First Love from Silhouette lost readers and ceased publication, while Sweet Valley High flourished. The second reason for the success of Sweet Valley High was the creation of spin-off series for younger and older readers featuring the same beloved characters. During the 1980s, the Sweet Valley universe expanded to include Sweet Valley Twins, Sweet Valley Kids, and The Unicorn Club.

During the 1980s, censorship of teen books and popular music frequently occurred. Young adult authors like Judy Blume and Norma Klein often had their books censored, and stories that contained sex were banned by parents, librarians, and schools. Even though the romance series contained minimal sexual content, many people still objected to the popularity of the romance renaissance. Librarians thought the books were fluffy trash, and many refused to carry them. Feminist critics argued that romance stories taught teenage girls to think about romance, love, and marriage rather than school, hobbies, and future plans for college and careers. During the 1980s, feminist activists continued to fight against sexism in society, and a few of these activists focused on the new teen romance novels in the early part of the decade.

Feminism, which had experienced a rebirth in the 1970s, was struggling to survive. The New Right was against social changes demanded by feminists, including sexual freedom for women, the proposed Equal Rights Amendment, affirmative action programs, and legalized abortion. Feminist critics abhorred the portrayal of girls and women in the new romance series.

But critics hadn't studied these titles closely, or they would have noted that many teen romances were actually coming-of-age stories in which girls were learning to balance friendships, romance and boyfriends, hobbies and extracurricular activities, and school, all while making plans to attend college and have careers. Rather than teaching girls to focus on love, marriage, and the baby carriage, many teen romance novels taught a generation of teenage girls that they could have it all—marriage, children, and careers. Teen romance fiction was training girls to become superwomen. The tensions and contradictions between 1970s feminism and 1980s conservative values can be found in teen romances published throughout the decade.

Such series books for preteens as Ann M. Martin's The Baby-Sitters Club also reflected these tensions. While seventh graders Kristy, Mary Anne, Stacey, and Claudia forge strong friendships and build their own business, they earn money babysitting. Feminist critiques of the series suggest that by promoting babysitting the series may encourage preteen and teen readers to focus on mothering as their primary goal in life. It can be said that The Baby-Sitters Club, like teen romance novels, taught girls that they could be superwomen with careers and family. As readers moved from the preteen friendship series to teen romances, this notion is reinforced.

Feminists objected to the conservative values found in the novels. Conservative values are clearly evident in the absence of sex in the early stories. Sex simply doesn't exist for the good girls in the contemporary romance series. Later in the decade, however, sex becomes an issue in teen romance fiction. Strangely, no one objected to this sexual content, even though there were concerns about the sexual activities in Judy Blume's books *Forever* and *Deenie* throughout the decade. In the Sweet Valley High series title *All Night Long*, Jessica gets involved with an older boy who expects her to have sex with him. When she says no, Scott threatens her with rape and verbally abuses her. But it is Jessica's fault for getting involved with an older boy and leading him on, the story implies. In a typical Sweet Valley High plot line, Elizabeth must save Jessica from herself, impersonating her sister while Jessica finds her way home. Jessica pretends she had a great time with Scott and his friends at their all-night party.

In the Sweet Valley universe, bad girls like Jessica are tempted to have sex, while good girls like Elizabeth hold hands with boys and share kisses that produce a few tingles. But since twins Jessica and Elizabeth are "two sides of the same person," Jessica can't have sex because Elizabeth won't have sex. Elizabeth must help Jessica rescue her reputation, because if she doesn't, her own reputation is sullied. While the Sweet Valley High series wasn't giving girls positive messages about sex, the series at least acknowledged that sex is an issue for teens. Everyone is thinking about it, and some young adults are actually having sex. By acknowledging that teens are sexual beings, Sweet Valley High outlasted all the other romance series introduced during the 1980s.

Mystery Series

Popular mystery series, like Nancy Drew and Trixie Belden, remained trendy with young adult readers. The Stratemeyer Syndicate's Kay Tracey series had another brief revival in 1980, when Bantam Books published six revised and updated books from the series. In the late 1970s, Stratemeyer Syndicate head Harriet Adams switched publishers, leaving Grosset & Dunlap for Simon & Schuster. Adams wanted to be paid more money for the Nancy Drew, Hardy Boys, and Bobbsey Twins series, but Grosset & Dunlap wanted to continue with the original agreement her father made with them forty years earlier. Simon & Schuster agreed to publish new titles in all three series and to market them more aggressively. Grosset & Dunlap shot back by suing the Stratemeyer Syndicate and Simon & Schuster for $300 million dollars, arguing that they shared copyright and ownership of the three series.

During the 1980 trial, many of the Stratemeyer Syndicate's secrets about the outlining, ghostwriting, and editing of their popular series were revealed. For many years, Adams claimed to be Carolyn Keene, author of the Nancy Drew stories. But Mildred Wirt, who after her first husband's death became Mildred Wirt Benson, who had ghostwritten many of the

original Nancy Drew stories, testified to her role in the creation and writing of the popular mystery series between 1929 and 1953. Grosset &
Dunlap won the rights to continue to reprint the 1950s revised Nancy
Drew and Hardy Boys titles they had already published, while the Stratemeyer Syndicate won the right to choose their future publisher.

By the time the trial took place, Simon & Schuster was already
working closely with the Stratemeyer Syndicate. In April 1980, Simon
& Schuster threw a lavish party to celebrate the fiftieth anniversary of
the Nancy Drew series, with Adams as the guest of honor. The party included the full cast of Nancy Drew characters and a mystery that had
to be solved by the end of the evening. Melanie Rehak reports, "Harriet was in mystery heaven."[21]

Simon & Schuster started publishing new Nancy Drew titles in paperback format in 1979. For the first few years, the new paperback stories resembled the Nancy Drew mysteries of the 1960s and 1970s. The
series continued after Adams's death in 1982 with more modern language and better pacing. In 1984, Adams's children and business partners sold the Stratemeyer Syndicate to Simon & Schuster. The vice
president and publisher of Simon & Schuster announced plans to update the Nancy Drew series: "We have to breathe new life into them. . . .
The characters are showing signs of age and need updating. Nancy . . .
doesn't reflect the realities of 1980s girlhood."[22]

A new series featuring Nancy and her friends, The Nancy Drew
Files, was introduced in 1986. This series was geared toward a slightly
older audience of readers in their early teens. While Nancy remains the
same strong, smart girl sleuth in both series, the settings and stories
changed to reflect contemporary teen culture. New settings, like ski re-
sorts, spas, dance clubs, and movie and music video sets, reflect the lavish lifestyle of middle and upper classes during the 1980s. Pivotal characters in the stories are entertainers, like rock stars, famous actors, and
well-known radio deejays or professional athletes.

Author Melanie Rehak that argues the new publisher "identified
'the interests and concerns of today's teens' . . . as boys and clothes and
the kind of superficial issues that the Nancy of old would never have
considered."[23] The publisher also licensed a line of clothing, accessories, and cosmetics aimed at girls between the ages of twelve and
eighteen called Nancy Drew's River Heights, USA.

Nancy Drew fans have also noted that the stories of the 1980s feature more adventure and romance than in the past. "Along with an obsession with fashion, modern Nancy Drew volumes feature murder, espionage, altered states, long kisses, and lots of passionate panting," Carole Kismaric and Marvin Heiferman contend.[24] In The Nancy Drew Files series, Nancy and her long-time boyfriend, Ned Nickerson, have an on-again, off-again relationship, leaving Nancy free to date other boys. Nancy's relationship with Ned is explained in the first book in the new series, *Secrets Can Kill*:

> Nancy and Ned had a very special relationship. They'd known each other since they were kids, and when they'd first realized they loved each other, they'd thought it would last forever. But neither one was ready for a "forever" commitment, so occasionally they drifted apart, dating other people.[25]

Nancy is surprised when Ned proposes marriage in 1988's *Till Death Do Us Part*, and she rejects the proposal. She is shocked to learn the very next day that Ned is engaged to another woman. Nancy is relieved when she learns that Ned proposed to Jessica Thorne only because he is suspicious of her interest in him, and he doesn't really intend to marry Jessica. Nancy and Ned investigate Jessica and discover that she wants to kill Ned, who resembles her missing husband, so she can inherit his aunt's estate. Nancy rescues Ned while flying an airplane, and the couple continues to date and solve mysteries together.

A spin-off series, River Heights, focused on the love lives of students at River Heights High School. In The Nancy Drew Files and River Heights, the publisher is clearly trying to market both Nancy Drew and teen romance together to compete with the many popular romance series. While River Heights only lasted a couple of years, The Nancy Drew Files were published for nine years.

Amateur sleuth Trixie Belden, along with her family and friends, continued to solve mysteries at home and abroad. In the early 1980s, Golden Press reissued older titles in the Trixie Belden series in paperback. New titles in the series were added to the paperback format in the first half of the decade. The later titles in the series were shorter and had larger font and illustrations, and the cast of characters appeared to be younger than in earlier titles, despite the fact that they aged only a year or two during the series run. The Western Publishing Company decided to cancel the series in 1986, because it didn't fit in with the other materials published by the company and because the series was not keeping up with the times. Melanie Knight reports, "Golden Press publicity manager Melanie Donovan stated that 'little girls today are a little more sophisticated . . . and prefer pseudosexy teen novels.'"[26] Knight points out that early Trixie Belden titles had light romantic story lines, and she argues that the series might have lasted longer if the publishing company hadn't decided to downplay romantic stories in later years. The Western Publishing Company did not rule out reprinting the series in the future.

The various Nancy Drew series were able to maintain popularity by changing to keep up with the times, while the Trixie Belden series ceased publication because the quaint rural settings and group of young friends were too old-fashioned. The inclusion of more romantic elements in the Nancy Drew series ensured their survival, while the exclusion of romance from Trixie Belden meant disaster.

The popularity and success of such teen romance series as Wildfire and Sweet Valley High was the most important publishing event of the decade. Teen romance fiction had an impact on the survival of popular mystery series Nancy Drew and Trixie Belden. Nancy endured, while Trixie vanished. Most romance series disappeared, too, but Sweet Valley High continued to dominate the teen book market. Even Sweet Valley High would be influenced by the next big trend in children's and young adult publishing—the horror novel.

Notes

1. Selma Lanes, "Here Come the Blockbusters—Teen Books Go Big Time," *Interracial Books for Children Bulletin*, 12 (1981): 5.

2. Patty Campbell, "Perplexing Young Adult Books: A Retrospective," *Wilson Library Bulletin*, 62 (1988): 26.

3. Linda Christian-Smith, *Becoming a Woman through Romance* (New York: Routledge, 1990), 2.

4. Victor Bondi, ed., *American Decades, 1980–1989* (Detroit: Gale Research, 1996), 425.

5. Lucy Rollin, *Twentieth-Century Teen Culture by the Decades* (Westport, CT: Greenwood, 1999), 271.

6. Michael Cart, *From Romance to Realism: 50 Years of Growth and Change in Young Adult Literature* (New York: HarperCollins, 1996), 106.

7. Wendy Smith, "An Earlier Start on Romance," *Publishers Weekly*, 220 (November 13, 1981): 58.

8. Pamela D. Pollack, "The Business of Popularity: The Surge of Teenage Paperbacks," *School Library Journal*, 28 (1981): 27.

9. Maud Johnson, *A Kiss for Tomorrow* (New York: Scholastic Book Services, 1981), 171.

10. Jane Claypool Miner, *Senior Class* (New York: Scholastic Book Services, 1982), 43–44.

11. Elaine Wagner, "Protesting Sexist Materials—You Can Make a Difference," *Interracial Books for Children*, 12.3 (1981), 3.

12. Pollack, "The Business of Popularity," 27.

13. Michael S. Barson, "Packaging for Romance Readers," *Publishers Weekly*, 220 (November 13, 1981): 52.

14. Anonymous, "$1.4 Million Targeted for Silhouette Teen Romances," *The Publishers Weekly*, 220 (November 13, 1981): 78.

15. Pollack, "The Business of Popularity," 28.

16. "Francine Pascal," in *Something about the Author: Volume 143* (Detroit, MI: Thomson Gale, 2004), 155.

17. Judith Appelbaum, "Paperback Talk: Joys and Pains of Packaging," *New York Times*, (November 27, 1983): BR 39–40.

18. Random House, "Meet Francine: Francine Pascal's SweetValley.com," www.randomhouse.com/sweetvalley/meetfrancine.html (accessed July 27, 2007).

19. M. Feitlowitz, "Interview with Francine Pascal," in *Authors and Artists for Young Adults* (Detroit: Gale Research, 1989), 198.

20. Mary M. Huntwork, "Why Girls Flock to Sweet Valley High," *School Library Journal*, 36 (1990): 137–38.

21. Melanie Rehak, *Girl Sleuth: Nancy Drew and the Women Who Created Her* (Orlando, FL: Harcourt, 2005), 294.

22. Rehak, *Girl Sleuth*, 300.

23. Rehak, *Girl Sleuth*, 300–301.

24. Carole Kismaric and Marvin Heiferman, *The Mysterious Case of Nancy Drew and the Hardy Boys* (New York: Fireside, 1998), 126.

25. Carolyn Keene, *Secrets Can Kill* (New York: Pocket Books, 1986), 4.

26. Melanie Knight, *Schoolgirl Shamuses, Inc.* (Rheem Valley, CA: SynSine, 1998), 42.

9

High School Horrors! Genre Fiction for Teens

Genre fiction continued to be popular with preteen and teen readers during the 1990s. Although the romance novel boom was over, such romance series as Sweet Dreams and soap opera series as Sweet Valley High remained in the teen book market. In the 1990s, the horror genre was popular in fiction and films, bolstered by the success of Stephen King's scary novels. Horror movies like *Scream, Halloween H20: 20 Years Later*, and two films based on Lois Duncan's teen thriller novel *I Know What You Did Last Summer* were popular in the second half of the decade. Such authors as R. L. Stine and Christopher Pike created tamer horror stories for children and teens, making horror novels the favorite genre with children and teen readers. Pike's Chain Letter series and Stine's Fear Street series, which blended mystery, horror, and thriller elements, were best sellers. While critics objected to the gory stories, teens gobbled them up. For teens who wanted their mysteries without the gore, Nancy Drew remained on the scene.

During the 1990s, a book packaging company called 17th Street Productions was responsible for the production of many teen book series. Founded by Jeffrey and Daniel Weiss as Cloverdale Press, the Weiss's spent the 1980s producing popular teen romance series like Sweet Valley High and Sweet Dreams. During the 1990s, the book packager changed its name to 17th Street Productions, packaging such popular series as SVH Senior Year, Sweet Valley Jr. High, and Fearless, all created by author Francine Pascal and written by ghostwriters.

The late 1990s saw stories of girl power appear on the market, fueled by popular televisions shows like *Buffy the Vampire Slayer* and *Charmed*. Francine Pascal's Fearless featured a teenage girl who becomes a vigilante crime fighter on the streets of New York City. By the early twenty-first century, both romance and horror fiction were passé. Instead, girl power series remained popular, with witchcraft becoming a popular theme in series like Sweep and T*Witches.

In 1999, Daniel Weiss sold 17th Street Productions to former employees Leslie Morgenstein and Ann Brashares, who in turn sold the company to Alloy, Inc., in 2000. Alloy focuses on youth media and marketing services, appealing to Generation Y to spend some of their disposable income on a variety of products, including books and clothes. By the middle of the decade, Alloy's entertainment division had a monopoly on the teen book series market, producing best sellers like the various Sweet Valley series, Fearless, Sweep, and Sisterhood of the Traveling Pants. Teen fiction borrowed a page from popular women's fiction, making teen chick lit the most popular genre of the decade with such series from Alloy as Gossip Girl, The It Girl, The A-List, and The Clique leading sales.

Finally, it is important to note that by the late twentieth and early twenty-first centuries, more preteen readers were reading teen series books. "The series books are popular, but with children becoming teenagers, not with the older teenagers whose lives are depicted in the books," notes teen literature expert Marc Aronson.[1] Most of the genre paperback series appealed to preteens or tweens, while some of the more literary chick lit series appealed to older teens.

Soap Opera and Romance Series

Although the teen romance boom of the 1980s was over, a few romance series survived into the 1990s and early twenty-first century. Bantam's Sweet Dreams morphed into the more modern Love Stories series, while Sweet Valley High continued to be extremely popular with teen and preteen readers. Sweet Valley High began publishing in trilogy format, with three books needed to tell one story. The series remained contemporary, keeping up with new technologies, fashions, and popular culture. Librarian Joyce Litton argues that *Sweet Valley High* developed a social conscience during the 1990s: "Sweet Valley High deals with quite a few contemporary social issues, including anorexia, date rape, disability, the sexism of beauty contests, racism, and a female quarterback."[2]

Sweet Valley High finally made it to television in 1994 as *Francine Pascal's Sweet Valley High*. Instead of a soap opera, however, the television series was a sitcom based on the books. Early shows relied heavily on the books for plots, but the show strayed farther from its origins and became sillier as it progressed. Francine Pascal's daughter, Jamie Stewart Carmen, did a terrific job casting twins Cynthia and Brittany Daniel as Elizabeth and Jessica. During the show's run, the Daniel twins were featured on the covers of the Sweet Valley High and Sweet Valley University book series. After a four-year run, the television series came to an end. Shortly afterward, the book series ceased publication. In the late 1990s, fictional teenagers were being portrayed as more sophisticated than the Wakefield twins, and young readers were losing interest in Sweet Valley High. The series ended with a three-book miniseries that included *Last Wish*, *Earthquake*, and *Aftershock*. In these final books, Sweet Valley experiences an earthquake on the eve of the Wakefield twins' seventeenth birthday that changes the lives of all the teens in Sweet Valley forever.

Francine Pascal's Sweet Valley University, a spin-off series, appeared in 1993. Sweet Valley University introduced new characters and plots aimed at older teen readers. Topics covered included relationships, marriage, date rape, alcohol, drugs, and sex. Although these books were popular with readers, critics did not like the series. Joyce Litton argues that, "young women are more likely to be portrayed as weak, resorting to feminine tricks to catch men, and rarely committed to . . . nontraditional careers."[3] For example, in *Wanted for Murder*, Elizabeth and Jessica pick up a homicidal hitchhiker, putting them on the FBI's most wanted list. The twins are rescued by Elizabeth's boyfriend Tom and the FBI. Joyce Litton suggests that Freshman Dorm and Nancy Drew on Campus portray young women as smarter, stronger, and more independent than the young women of Sweet Valley University. Moreover, she says, "Sweet Valley University does not have a well-defined social conscience."[4]

I disagree with Litton. Some books in the series deal with peer pressure to be sexually active, some address date rape, and others address sex in a positive way. For instance, Elizabeth rescues Jessica from date rapist James Montgomery in *No Means No*. Jessica, who was briefly married to Mike McAllery in *A Married Woman*, helps readers understand that they can say no to sex even if they have already been sexually active. Elizabeth, on the other hand, has several boyfriends throughout the series who pressure her for sex. In *Elizabeth in Love*, Elizabeth decides she is ready to have sex with her boyfriend Sam, but he wants to wait. In the Elizabeth series published in 2001, after Elizabeth sees Jessica kissing Sam, she runs away to England, where she falls in love with aristocrat Max Pennington. Elizabeth finally has sex for the first time in the ironically titled *Max's Choice*. In the Sweet Valley University and Elizabeth series, the Wakefield twins and their friends learn to be responsible while becoming sexually active.

In 1998, Pascal introduced the sophisticated and edgier Francine Pascal's SVH Senior Year series for teens and Francine Pascal's Sweet Valley Jr. High for tweens. SVH Senior Year follows the Wakefield twins and their new friends through their senior year of high school. Although the series tried hard to include a more diverse cast of characters, including gay, Hispanic, and African American teens, the books faltered. Attempts to update the lead characters, Elizabeth and Jessica Wakefield, failed miserably. Pascal and her ghostwriters tried to swap the twins' personalities to show character development, but the move confused long-time fans of the series.

In a farewell letter in the last book, *Sweet 18*, Francine Pascal contends that the series focused on girls' lives beyond romance: "Girls, not boys, drove the action. And there was plenty of action. Not just romance, but exciting things happening. Just like in real life. In fact, Sweet Valley is a microcosm of the real world."[5] Perhaps SVH Senior Year failed to attract readers because the series creator tried to change Sweet Valley from fantasy to reality. Pascal, however, does not rule out a Sweet Valley revival: "Perhaps in a few years, I'll start again with a Sweet Valley for the twenty-first century."[6]

Indeed, Pascal launched several revised titles in the original Sweet Valley High series in 2008. Updates to the stories include such new technologies as cell phones, the Internet, blogs, and text and instant messaging. Designer clothing, makeup, and accessories, along with many brand names and current popular culture references, put Elizabeth and Jessica Wakefield firmly in the twenty-first century. A controversial change includes the Wakefield twins' smaller dress size, sparking heated debates on the Internet about the impact of the books on girls' eating habits and body image. Instead of being a size six, Jessica and Elizabeth are now a "perfect-size-four."[7] In a brilliant move, Random House tapped teen soap opera actress and New York It Girl Leven Rambin, who plays the dual role of good girl Lily and her bad girl half-sister, Ava, on *All My Children*, to model as the Wakefield twins on the book covers and the promotional website.

Altogether, the various series in the Sweet Valley universe published more than 700 titles and sold 250 million copies in 25 languages over twenty years. Creator Francine Pascal earned $15 million from the series, despite the fact that she never actually wrote any of the books.[8] Random House is banking on the fact that an updated Sweet Valley High series will appeal to contemporary teens and tweens, but only time will tell if Pascal can repeat her success and compete with such popular chick lit series as Gossip Girl and The Clique.

Horror Novels

Teen horror novels first entered the book market in the mid-1980s, when Christopher Pike (a pseudonym used by Kevin McFadden) published *Slumber Party*, the story of six teens who experience strange and violent events while trapped in a winter vacation home during a blizzard. Pike went on to become a best-selling teen horror author in the 1990s, publishing both single titles and such series as Chain Letter, Final Friends, The Last Vampire, and Spooksville. In the Chain Letter series, a group of friends get taunting letters from someone who knows their secrets. By 1994, Pike had nine million books in print.[9] While Pike's teen horror stories continue to be reissued, Pike recently changed gears and began writing fantasy series for teens, for instance the Alosha Trilogy.

R. L. Stine also found tremendous success writing horror series for children and teens. Like Pike, Stine started writing for teens in the late 1980s, when Pocket Books created the Crosswinds romance and mystery series to replace First Love from Silhouette. *Broken Date*, a Crosswinds title by Stine, is a romantic thriller about high school seniors Jamie and Tom. Everything goes wrong for Jamie the day Tom breaks a date—she witnesses a crime, she is stalked, and she believes her boyfriend might be a killer. Shortly after writing for the Crosswinds series, Stine created two horror series, the best-selling Goosebumps series for children, and the Fear Street series for teen readers. Fear Street focuses on a scary part of the town of Shadyside, near the abandoned Fear mansion and the graveyard, where ghosts and skeletons reside.

In *The New Girl*, the first book in the Fear Street series, Corey falls in love with Anna, but when Corey tries to contact Anna, her family informs him that she is dead. Corey finally learns the girl he believes is Anna is really her mentally ill sister, who killed Anna and took over her identity. The Fear Street stories are suspenseful, with a clumsy dash of mystery and romance added to the tame horror elements. For instance, Brady is recovering from the tragic loss of his girlfriend, Sharon, in a sledding accident, when he meets Rosha in *The Perfect Date*. Although Brady is still haunted by the sight of Sharon's mangled body, he falls in love with Rosha, but he can't find Rosha at home or school. Instead, he keeps finding a scarred girl who tells him that Rosha wants to kill him. The story ends with Rosha revealing she is Sharon, back from the dead in another girl's body.

The Fear Street stories are filled with dead people, ghosts, skeletons, murders, and a bit of gore. Several spin-off series, including Fear Street Cheerleaders, Fear Street Sagas, Fear Street Seniors, Fear Street Super Chillers, Ghosts of Fear Street, and 99 Fear Street, were popular throughout the 1990s, making Fear Street "the best-selling young adult book series in history."[10] Stine's horror empire came crashing down in the late 1990s when his wife's packaging company, Parachute Press, and Scholastic Books became involved in a bitter legal battle over the profits from the sales of Stine's popular Goosebumps series.

Nevertheless, Stine continues to write horror stories for children and teens. In 2000, Stine began a new teen series called The Nightmare Room, which was turned into a television show in 2001. In this series, teens accidentally end up in The Nightmare Room, where terrifying things happen to them. Stine also launched a new Fear Street series called Fear Street Nights in June 2005. Teens hang out at the popular nightclub called Nights, built on the location of the old Fear mansion.

The success of Goosebumps earned Stine a place in the *Guinness World Records 2000 Millennium Edition* as the author of the top-selling children's book series. The *Goosebumps* television show, which ran from 1995 to 1998, was the number one children's show in the United States for three years.[11] Altogether, there are more than 300 million copies of Stine's books in print.[12] Horror was, without a doubt, the most popular genre of books for children and teens at the end of the twentieth century.

Mystery Series

Popular girls' mystery series remained on the scene, and in the 1990s, Nancy Drew got another makeover. Launched in 1995, the Nancy Drew on Campus series was more soap opera romance than mystery. For instance, in *New Lives, New Loves*, Nancy is more concerned about her long-distance relationship with Ned Nickerson than ever before, but she reminds herself throughout the story that she chose to attend a different university than him: "If she went to Emerson, she knew she'd be walking in Ned's shadow."[13] Although she is finally a college student, Nancy is no longer the spunky, independent young woman known to readers. Throughout the first story, Nancy believes that Ned is getting in the way of her studies, social life, and mystery solving at Wilder University. Ned, on the other hand, gets upset that Nancy no longer has time for him. Nancy and Ned's relationship is rocky in this series, and Nancy often dates other young men. The series is very similar to its contemporary, Sweet Valley University, with a mystery thrown into every story.

The mysteries in this series are simple, yet Nancy often has trouble solving them. "Mystery is still a part of her life, but Nancy seems to have forgotten everything she ought to have learned from her extensive experience."[14] This new Nancy often comes across as dumb, missing easy clues she wouldn't have missed in previous series. Nancy, Bess, and George all make new friends, shifting the focus from the trio of friends to a wider social circle. Although George has sex with her boyfriend, Will Blackfeather, they refrain from sexual activity after a pregnancy scare. The Nancy Drew on Campus series abruptly ceased publication in 1998 after three years. A 2002 Disney television movie, *Nancy Drew*, based on this series starred Maggie Lawson as a first-year college student at River Heights University. Clearly this was a pilot for a new *Nancy Drew* television show, but no television series materialized.

Publisher Simon & Schuster continued to add new titles to the original Nancy Drew Mystery Series until 2003. In these stories, Nancy Drew continues to be portrayed as smart, assertive, and independent. Cousins Bess Marvin and George Fayne still accompany Nancy on her adventures. In the last book in the series, *Werewolf in a Winter Wonderland*, Nancy and her friends are called upon to solve the mysteries of a werewolf frightening people at Winter Carnival and the disappearance of wolves from a wildlife preserve. Although Nancy is still dating Ned, she can usually find her own way out of trouble by keeping her wits about her and using her brains to solve problems.

In the early twenty-first century, several new versions of Nancy Drew were introduced for younger readers. In 2004, Nancy Drew, Girl Detective brought Nancy Drew and her friends to readers in grades four through seven, while Nancy Drew and the Clue Crew introduces younger readers to Nancy and the gang. The Nancy Drew, Girl Detective graphic novel series was launched in 2005 to take advantage of the popularity of graphic novels. By the early twenty-first century, all the different Nancy Drew series were aimed at preteen readers rather than teens.

A new Nancy Drew movie aimed at tweens, starring Emma Roberts from the Nickelodeon Channel's television show *Unfabulous*, was released in theaters in the summer of 2007. In this version of the story, young Nancy travels to Hollywood, where her old-fashioned ways make her a misfit at school. Her father wants her to give up sleuthing and become a normal teenager, but Nancy can't stop solving mysteries, and living in the haunted house of a murdered movie star presents her with several mysteries, including an unsolved murder, a missing will, and a long-lost heir. The old-fashioned Nancy charms everyone; she solves the mysteries and returns to her comfortable life in River Heights.

Other popular mystery series were revived in the early twenty-first century. In 2003, Random House brought Trixie Belden back into print. Aimed at readers ages nine through twelve, the Trixie Belden books feature new cover art with the original stories. Between 2005 and 2007, sixteen titles originally published in the Cherry Ames career and mystery series were reissued by Spring Publishing Company, a publisher specializing in academic and professional titles. Editor Harriet Schulman Forman wanted to "bring Cherry Ames back so a whole new generation of readers could enjoy the adventures and values of Helen Wells's plucky heroine and perhaps even be inspired, as [she] had been, to choose nursing as their life's work," since there was a shortage of registered nurses in the United States.[15] It is interesting to note that the series was reprinted at a time when the United States is fighting wars in Iraq and Afghanistan, since early books in the series feature Cherry working as an army nurse during World War II. Despite the serious and scary nature of the first few books in the series set during World War II, Forman believes that children today will enjoy reading the Cherry Ames series, and they may even think about nursing as a career. In the twenty-first century, popular mystery series are aimed at preteen rather than teen readers, and while most of the series are light and entertaining reads, the revival of a series like Cherry Ames might help readers learn about more serious issues, for example war and careers.

Girl Power Series

When activist and author Rebecca Walker coined the term "third wave" feminism in the early 1990s, she enabled young women to redefine feminism as more inclusive and more active than the liberal and radical feminisms popular in the 1970s and 1980s. Third wave feminism brought girl power to popular culture, including series books featuring girls with extraordinary physical strength or special powers, for instance the ability to perform Wiccan magic. The *Oxford English Dictionary* defines girl power as "a self-reliant attitude among girls and young women manifested in ambition, assertiveness, and individualism."[16] Girl power began appearing everywhere, from such television shows as *Buffy the Vampire Slayer* and *Powerpuff Girls* to music groups like the Spice Girls, who used "Girl Power!" as their slogan. Emilie Zaslow argues, however, that girl power has two meanings that are sometimes contradictory:

Girl power can be seen in two distinct, yet overlapping, ways: as a watered-down feminist position available as a stylish accessory, and as a popularized yet meaningful and widespread embodiment of some third-wave feminist positions.[17]

Girl power, with all its contradictions, was a popular theme in girls' series books published in the late twentieth and early twenty-first centuries. Some girl power stories feature young women with physical strength and martial arts skills, while other series feature girls with unusual abilities, like magical powers. Francine Pascal, creator of the Sweet Valley books, created a new series called Fearless about a teenage girl who was born without the fear gene. Gaia Moore, a high school misfit, lives with a family friend and hangs around the streets of New York City after her mother is murdered and her CIA agent father abandons her. When Gaia discovers that New York is a dangerous place, she uses her lack of fear and martial arts skills to make the city safer for everyone. In *Gone*, the final book in the series, Gaia graduates from high school and leaves New York City. A television movie based on the Fearless series aired in 2004, but as Francine Pascal pointed out in an interview, the television series *Dark Angel* had already made the Fearless story popular on television: "The big one is *Dark Angel*—[series creator] James Cameron just stole it. . . . And I guess he could—he's the *Titanic* 'king of the world' man."[18]

While no authorized television series based on Fearless appeared, Gaia's story picks up again in the Fearless FBI series. In *Kill Game*, the FBI recruits Gaia after she stops a suicide bomber intent on killing everyone at her university graduation. Gaia goes to Quantico for an FBI training program, where she becomes involved in a fake murder investigation. While Gaia was strong and empowered in the original Fearless series, Fearless FBI portrays her as a young woman with psychological problems that threaten her new career with the FBI, clearly showing the contradictory definitions of girl power in popular culture. Whether it was intentional, the Gaia portrayed in Fearless FBI is intelligent and physically strong but psychologically weak. In this context, Fearless FBI can be interpreted as a backlash against third-wave feminism.

Nonetheless, Pascal has succeeded in creating an interesting mystery series for older teen readers with well developed characters, including smart, career-oriented young women. Both Fearless and Fearless FBI are packaged by Alloy, Inc. Another Alloy series, Samurai Girl, features nineteen-year-old Heaven Kogo, a Japanese woman whose life is turned upside down when her beloved brother is killed by ninjas during her wedding ceremony in Hollywood. Although this series tried to emulate the action and suspense of the Fearless series, the story ended abruptly after six books.

Witchcraft is another popular girl power theme. Author Cate Tiernan, a pseudonym for Gabrielle Charbonnet, launched the Sweep series in 2001, with *Book of Shadows*. In this first book in the series, Morgan Rowlands learns about witchcraft from a new boy at school. Morgan soon discovers that she is a very powerful blood witch and that she must save the world from evil witches. Although the series had a loyal group of fans, it was cancelled after fifteen books. In 2005, Tiernan published the Balefire series, a story about reunited teen twins who are witches. Members of the Treize coven, who are immortal, fear the power of twin witches Clio and Thais, and they try to harm the twins before they discover the extent of their power. Another series with a similar premise is T*Witches, where reunited twins Cam and Alex discover that they are witches. In 2005, Disney produced a television movie based on T*Witches, starring Tia and Tamera Mowry. Fans of the television show *Charmed* enjoy these book series focusing on magic and witchcraft.

Chick Lit Series

With the demise of soap opera romances and horror series in the late 1990s, the teen series book market was due for a change. The girl power series were just not as popular as these previous genres. Chick lit, which became popular with adult readers with Helen Fielding's *Bridget Jones's Diary*, fit the bill. While women's chick lit focuses on the social lives and relationships of young professional women, teen chick lit focuses on social and class status of girls in high school, often pitting the popular, rich Queen Bee against the ordinary misfit girl. British chick lit series for teens and tweens, for example Louise Rennison's Confessions of Georgia Nicolson books and Cathy Hopkins's Mates, Dates, and . . . series, became popular in the United States in the early twenty-first century.

Soon American teen chick lit was everywhere. Single title books like Meg Cabot's *The Princess Diaries*, Ann Brashares's *Sisterhood of the Traveling Pants*, and Megan McCafferty's *Sloppy Firsts* were turned into series because of their popularity. Alloy, Inc. replaced the Sweet Valley series with several popular chick lit series, including Gossip Girl by Cecily Von Ziegesar, The A-List by Zoey Dean, and The Clique by Lisi Harrison. "In this post-9/11 world where there is so much uncertainty about the future, it is no surprise that escapist literature has exploded," argues library media specialist Christine Meloni.[19]

Cecily Von Ziegesar, an editor who worked for book packager 17th Street Productions, conceived Gossip Girl as the teen version of the television show *Sex and the City*. Von Ziegesar set the series in upper-crust New York City prep schools, a world she knew well from experience. Main characters include mean, insecure, virginal Blair Waldorf; flaky, beautiful golden girl Serena van der Woodsen; and Nate Archibald, the stoner boy loved by both Blair and Serena. They are the modern versions of teens Veronica, Betty, and Archie from the *Archie* comics. Filmmaker Vanessa, her tortured poet boyfriend, Dan, and his little sister, Jenny, who will do anything to become popular, are also part of the cast of characters. Gossip Girl, the bitchy star of the series, is an anonymous character who writes a blog gossiping about the cast of characters in the series. He or she signs each entry in his/her blog with the signature, "You know you love me." In this gossipy series, no topic is off limits, and the young characters engage in sex, drinking, and drugs on a regular basis. The behavior of the characters is so outrageous, in fact, that the author seems to be making fun of them as she tells their stories.

After Gossip Girl sold to Little, Brown and Company, Alloy executives asked Von Ziegesar to write the series. While it makes sense to assume that the writer who conceives the idea actually writes the series, this is not how Alloy works. For instance, Alloy editor Jodi Anderson came up with the idea for the Sisterhood of the Traveling Pants series, but she wasn't asked to write the books. Instead, other writers were approached.[20] In the end, Alloy executive and former co-owner of 17th Street Productions Ann Brashares chose to write the best-selling series about the special pants that keep friends Tibby, Lena, Bridget, and Carmen connected during their separate summer vacations. One author who worked for the book packaging company reports, "They have writers who don't exist, and they have writers who don't really write the stuff, and they have series supposedly by one author that are by many. There's no one-to-one alignment between anything that gets produced and the producer."[21] According to 17th Street president Leslie Morgenstein,

> We are very collaborative with our authors. We work with them to develop stories and outlines and then provide extensive feedback on manuscripts. In the case of Cecily and Gossip Girl, she is much more in the driver's seat then [sic] our team here. We are more of a sounding board, providing feedback, then [sic] a resource that is handing her story or outline to write from.[22]

Although Von Ziegesar is credited as the author on the first eight books in the Gossip Girl series, *The Harvard Independent Online* reports, "she does not write every word within" the books.[23] Von Ziegesar contends, "People don't really get it—it's such an unusual way to create books. But I'm very much the writer of my books, the final product is very much mine."[24] That is until book number nine, *Only in Your Dreams*, when ghostwriters permanently took over the series. Morgenstein asserts, "Cecily doesn't and never has owned the concept. . . . She is a financial participant but does not control or have ownership in the underlying rights [to the series]."[25] Journalist Emily Nussbaum gossips, "She'd love to end the series; she knows it's not hers to end."[26] One wonders why Von Ziegesar would want to end such a successful series. By early 2007, there were 4.5 million Gossip Girl books in print.[27]

The original Gossip Girl series finally ended in 2007 with *Don't You Forget about Me*, and in the last line of the book, readers finally find out Gossip Girl's identity. A quick review of reader's comments at Amazon.com indicates, however, that the solution to the mystery is so subtle that many readers missed it. Of course, Alloy continues the successful series with prequels featuring the original characters and a whole new cast of Gossip Girl characters, starring the Carlyle triplets, Owen, Peyton, and Baby.[28] Despite the ending of the original Gossip Girl series, the CW television network launched a prime-time drama based on the books in 2007, starring Blake Lively, Leighton Meester, and Chace Crawford as Serena, Blair, and Nate, repsectively. The character of Gossip Girl is played in voice-overs by Kristin Bell, who starred in the

CW network's popular series *Veronica Mars*. Since many readers didn't recognize Gossip Girl's identity in *Don't You Forget about Me*, the television show continues to keep fans guessing: "[T]he central mystery remains—who is Gossip Girl?"[29]

Ghostwriters also write The It Girl series, a spin-off that sends Gossip Girl character Jenny Humphrey to boarding school.[30] When Jenny arrives at Waverly Academy, she rivals popular Tinsley for the title of campus It Girl. Von Ziegesar is credited as creator, rather than author, of The It Girl and as creator of later titles in the Gossip Girl series. In an article in *New York* magazine, Emily Nussbaum reports that Von Ziegesar oversees Gossip Girl and contributes to The It Girl. While Von Ziegesar is credited as author of *It Had to Be You*, a Gossip Girl prequel published in October 2007, the author distances herself from the book in a message posted on Amazon.com:

> I just want all my readers to know that the GG prequel, *It Had to Be You*, *was* really great, and I *was* really proud of it, until the copyeditors and proofreaders changed words that shouldn't have been changed and created mistakes in the book that shouldn't be there. I worked really hard and spent a year writing the book, and I was so excited when it finally came out, but now I just want everyone to read the book I wrote, not the tampered-with version.[31]

In Private, another boarding school series produced by Alloy and written by Kate Brian, a pseudonym for young adult author Kieran Scott, Reed Brennan learns the secrets of the popular Billings Girls at Easton Academy, and she desperately wants to become a Billings Girl. While The It Girl and Private both begin with the "new girl who wants to be popular" theme, Private evolves into a delicious murder mystery. Reed Brennan, however, is no Nancy Drew. Instead, working-class Reed finds many mysteries, both big and small, in the world of wealthy mean girls and messed up rich boys, including the murder of her first lover, Thomas Pearson. One seriously doubts insecure Reed's abilities to solve the mystery and walk away from the nasty, shallow Billings Girls.

In the fourth book in the series, *Confessions*, Reed finally begins to think for herself, and she solves the murder mystery. The Private series continues, hopefully with a stronger protagonist and more exciting mysteries. It seems boarding school mystery series, which have been mostly absent from the teen book market during the last few decades, are making a comeback. But they look different from similar series of earlier decades, with their focus being on consumption of everything from goods, like clothing and electronics, to the very characters themselves.

In The A-List series, wealthy Anna Percy moves to Los Angeles to live with her father after her sister goes into drug rehab, her mother takes off to Europe, and her best friend hooks up with the boy she loves. Amidst the glitz and glam of L.A., Anna meets sometimes friends Cammie, Sam, and Dee and sometimes boyfriend Ben. Author Zoey Dean is "a pseudonym for an unknown married writing team" hired by Alloy to write the series.[32] Lisi Harrison, on the other hand, was an author wannabe who was invited to write The Clique series. Harrison worked at MTV "when she was approached by Alloy to create books about wealthy, junior-high queen bees."[33] Wealthy tween queen Massie Block and her Westchester, Connecticut, clique struggle with the idea of becoming friends with middle-class Claire Lyons. Since the series is aimed at preteens rather than teens, the romantic relationships are limited to crushes and first kisses. This series focuses on class status in middle school and society. A careful look at the acknowledgments in the books indicates that ghostwriters may be working with Harrison on the series. In 2007, Alloy hosted a contest for readers to win a role in a movie based on The Clique series, due out in theaters in 2008.

Such chick lit series as Gossip Girl, The Clique, and The A-List feature shallow young women who are consumers of everything—the most expensive food, drink, drugs, technological gadgets, clothing, makeup, and accessories their parents' money can buy. "[B]rands are so prominent you wonder if there are product placement deals," speculates Naomi Wolf.[34] She may be right. Amy Pattee notes the branding of the series themselves:

> It is especially interesting to examine how the new Alloy series operate as brands of a sort by referring back to each other in peritextual promotions and seem to rely on each other to grant status or confer worth among readers. Just as the series characters use brands and branding to identify and value each other, the It Girl and The A List will use the value of Gossip Girl and Alloy, Inc. to establish their own symbolic value.[35]

An amusing example of this is Glossip Girl lip gloss, which Massie Block orders online in The Clique. Just as readers consume the series produced by Alloy, Inc., the girls in the stories consume other people, including friends, boys, and adults, to get what they want. When adults are present, they are only there for the money and gifts that they can bestow upon their children. As in the movie *Mean Girls*, characters are "frenemies"—sometimes friends, sometimes enemies. Boys, conversely, are often used and then tossed aside. For instance, Gossip Girl Serena goes through young men like bubblegum, while her "frenemy" Blair slowly learns to hook up with a new boy every week. Journalist Laura Sessions Stepp defines contemporary teen hook up culture:

> Hooking up can consist entirely of one kiss, or it can involve fondling, oral sex, anal sex, intercourse, or any combination of those things. It can happen only once with a partner, several times during a week, or over many months. Partners may know each other well, only slightly, or not at all, even after they have hooked up regularly. A hookup often happens in a bedroom, although other places will do: dance floors, bars, bathrooms, auditoriums, or any deserted room on campus. . . . It can mean the start of something, the end of something, or the whole of something.[36]

In the stories, like in real life, girls simply move on when they are bored with their boy toys. Sex has become a game for the middle-class and upper-class kids of the Millennial generation, who are too busy with school and extracurricular activities to have time for real relationships. "In both high school and college, the hallmark of hooking up is that the boy, once recruited, is disposable. . . . There's no such thing as cultivating the relationship," argues Stepp.[37] Gossip Girl reflects this culture of sexual consumption, along with the consumption of brand name products. "The raison d'etre of the Gossip Girl characters involves consumption and display; coincidentally, this observation can be made about the series—as a literary product—itself," notes Amy Pattee.[38]

Wolf argues, "The problem [with the books] is a value system in which meanness rules, parents check out, conformity is everything, and stressed-out adult values are presumed to be meaningful to teenagers."[39] This is true. "But all of this is presented in such an exaggerated way that no sensible teen would take it for anything but the silly wish-fulfillment fantasy it is," Patty Campbell contends.[40] One would certainly hope that readers don't take teen chick lit too seriously. Campbell points out, "Even at its worst, chick lit is *fun*, a fact ignored by solemn critics like me and Naomi Wolf."[41]

Not only are chick lit series fun to read, they actually *make fun* of the young women characters they claim to celebrate. This points to a darker side of teen chick lit that has been noted by critics. "First, let us acknowledge that the term [chick lit] itself is inherently demeaning, perhaps even sexist. *Chick* is a derogatory reference to the presumably air-headed girls or young women who are both the characters and the readers; *lit* is an ironic reference to the assumed lack of quality writing in the form."[42] The tone of teen chick lit is sometimes very harsh, with the narrator or author clearly making fun of the outrageous characters in the stories. Rather than celebrating the teen characters, chick lit series often debase young women. Wolf argues, "Since women have been writing for and about girls, the core of the tradition has been the opposition between the rebel and the popular, often wealthy anti-heroine."[43]

Women, however, have not necessarily created or written many series books supposedly authored by women for girls in the early twenty-first century. Instead, ghostwriters whose sex is unknown write stories for girls created and designed by men. For instance, media reports indicate that many executives at Alloy Entertainment are men. Writer John Barlow refers to them as "the Sweet Valley boys."[44] Teen chick lit, most especially the books produced by Alloy, may be demeaning because young females are portrayed the way men see them, rather than as women see them. Pattee suggests, "If Gossip Girl is really Gossip Boy, his critiques take on a distinctly different flavor as we consider the power of the female gaze versus the male gaze."[45] One mother notes, "You go to the teen-lit shelf and the boy books are sci-fi and fantasy books. . . . The girls books are about cliques and boyfriends. I don't think society grooms girls to be achievers the same way it grooms boys to be achievers."[46] Indeed, Gossip Girl's Blair Waldorf is desperate to get into Yale University, but readers don't get a sense of her career plans. Her sometimes friend Serena, a character likely based on celebutante Paris Hilton, has already succeeded as a model and an actress without any effort on her part. Men literally fall at Serena's feet, begging her to model their clothing and perfume lines or to star in their movies and music videos, and her picture is always on buses, billboards, and magazines all over New York City.

Even author Francine Pascal, who has been Alloy's most popular author for many years, has expressed concern about the content of recent books produced by the packager. Pascal notes, "Emotionally, there's no progress. . . . It doesn't touch on the classic values that Sweet Valley did—love, loyalty, friendship."[47] It is rather ironic that Gossip Girl creator, author, and editor Cecily Von Ziegesar spoke out on Amazon.com about editorial mistakes in her Gossip Girl prequel *It Had to Be You* rather than addressing her critics.

Chick lit series written by one author, rather than ghostwriters, also became popular in the early twenty-first century. Meg Cabot's The Princess Diaries series follows Princess Mia Thermopolis through the trials and tribulations of learning how to behave like the princess she didn't know she was. While she deals with the unusual and often humorous problems of life as a princess, Mia is also trying to lead the life of an ordinary high school student with her friends and boyfriend. The success of the series was assured with the release of two Disney movies, *The Princess Diaries* and *Princess Diaries 2: Royal Engagement*. Cabot publishes one or two books in the series each year, and she plans to see Mia through high school. Cabot also writes the popular paranormal teen series The Mediator, about a girl who can communicate with ghosts, and 1-800-Where-R-You, about a teen psychic who works with the FBI. 1-800-Where-R-You was a short-lived television show in the early twenty-first century on the Lifetime Network called *1-800-Missing* and later *Missing*. Cabot, who also writes single-title chick lit stories for women and teens, is the current queen of popular teen fiction.

Author Megan McCafferty wanted to write a more literary novel about a girl in high school, so she created nerdy Jessica Darling, who is trying to cope with life after her best friend moves away in *Sloppy Firsts*. Jessica befriends Marcus Flutie, an older boy who is known for doing drugs and sleeping around. *Second Helpings*, *Charmed Thirds*, and *Fourth Comings* continue the story of Jessica and Marcus's maturing romance while they finish high school, attend a university, and enter the workforce. The Jessica Darling stories have a harder, more cynical edge than The Princess Diaries series and are aimed at an older teen audience. In 2006, McCafferty's books became world renowned after McCafferty and her publisher, Crown, accused teen author Kaavya Viswanathan of plagiarizing more than forty passages from *Sloppy Firsts* and *Second Helpings* in her book *How Opal Mehta Got Kissed, Got Wild, and Got a Life*. Viswanathan's book was pulled from the market after further plagiarism allegations, including one passage from Meg Cabot's *The Princess Diaries*, were reported to the American media. Alloy co-owns the copyright on Viswanathan's book, and although the company admits to working with Viswanathan to shape the story, they deny any involvement in the plagiarism of other authors' works. Nevertheless, Alloy's book packaging practices became big news. The plagiarism scandal came to an end when Viswanathan's publisher, Little, Brown, pulled the book from the market in May 2006, less than a month after it was published.

While horror fiction was popular with preteens and teens in the 1990s, chick lit is the latest genre to gain popularity with these readers. The genres continue to blend together, with boarding school stories, mysteries, romances, college stories, and girl power series mixing with teen chick lit. With book sales for readers ages twelve and up rising by 23 percent in the early twenty-first century, "young adult fiction . . . is one of the book industry's healthiest segments."[48] Girls' series books, which have been around for more than 160 years, continue to be an important part of the teen book market.

Although critics have objected to the content and lack of character development found in girls' series books for more than a century and a half, teen and preteen girls enjoy reading contemporary girls' series because they regard them as contemporary fantasy stories. Girls' series books generally feature middle-class and upper-class girls who have everything any girl could want, including indulgent parents who give her the latest fashions and current technological gadgets, a big house, opportunities to travel, and the adoration of everyone she meets, whether the girl is Elsie Dinsmore, Nancy Drew, Sweet Valley High stars Elizabeth and Jessica, or Gossip Girls Blair and Serena. Most of the protagonists in popular girls' series books live a fantasy life that, for most readers, is only a dream world. Girls will likely continue to enjoy spending time with their favorite fictional sisters, schoolgirls, and sleuths, reading about their lives, loves, and adventures in girls' series books for many more years.

Notes

1. Marc Aronson, *Exploding the Myths: The Truth about Teenagers and Reading* (Lanham, MD: Scarecrow, 2001), 58.

2. Joyce Litton, "The Sweet Valley Gang Goes to College," *The ALAN Review*, 24.1 (1996), http://scholar.lib.vt.edu/ejournals/ALAN/fall96/f96-06-Litton.html (accessed April 27, 2006).

3. Litton, "The Sweet Valley Gang Goes to College."

4. Litton, "The Sweet Valley Gang Goes to College."

5. Francine Pascal, *Sweet 18* (New York: Bantam Books, 2003), 183.

6. Pascal, *Sweet 18*, 183.

7. Kate William, *Double Love* (New York: Laurel-Leaf, 2008), 1.

8. Chana R. Schoenberger, "A Valley Girl Grows Up," *Forbes*, 170 (October 28, 2002): 114.

9. Patty Campbell, "The Sand in the Oyster," *Horn Book*, 70.2 (March 1994): 237.

10. R. L. Stine, "R. L. Stine Official Website: Author Biography," www.rlstine.com/home.php (accessed on July 27, 2006).

11. Stine, "R. L. Stine Official Website: Author Biography."

12. Paul Gray, "Another Stab at Chills!" *Time*, 156.9 (August 28, 2000): 56–58, http://proquest.umi.com (accessed July 24, 2006).

13. Carolyn Keene, *New Lives, New Loves* (New York: Pocket Books, 1995), 6.

14. Society of Phantom Friends, *The Girls' Series Companion* (Rheem Valley, CA: SynSine, 1997), 388.

15. "An Interview with Harriet Schulman Forman," *Springer Publishing Company*, www.springerpub.com/default.aspx?pid=92 (accessed July 18, 2007).

16. *Oxford English Dictionary Online* (Oxford, U.K.: Oxford University Press, 2006), http://dictionary.oed.com (accessed July 28, 2006).

17. Emilie Zaslow, "Girl Power," *The Women's Movement Today: An Encyclopedia of Third-Wave Feminism*, ed. Leslie L. Heywood (Westport, CT: Greenwood, 2006), 161.

18. Kristin Kloberdanz, "Fear Factor," *Book*, 23 (July/August 2002): 30.

19. Christine Meloni, "Teen Chick Lit," *Library Media Connection*, 25.2 (2006): 16.

20. Sheelah Kolhatkar, "Viswanathan-athon: Plagiarizing Writer Fell in Weird Alloy," *The New York Observer* (May 8, 2006), www.observer.com/printpage.asp?iid=12761&ic=News+story+1 (accessed May 4, 2006).

21. Kolhatkar, "Viswanathan-athon."

22. Amy Pattee, "Commodities in Literature, Literature as Commodity: A Close Look at the Gossip Girl Series," *Children's Literature Association Quarterly*, 31.2 (2006): 163.

23. Shane Wilson, "Did Opal Author Plagiarize—Or Was It Her Handlers?" *The Harvard Independent Online*, www.harvardindependent.com/ViewArticle .aspx?ArticleID=9906 (accessed April 24, 2006).

24. Wilson, "Did Opal Author Plagiarize—Or Was It Her Handlers?"

25. Pattee, "Commodities in Literature, Literature as Commodity," 163.

26. Emily Nussbaum, "Psst, Serena is a Slut. Pass It On," *New York*, 38.19 (2005): 43.

27. Shannon Maughan, "Gossip Girl's Got Legs," *Publisher's Weekly*, 254.20 (May 14, 2007): 21.

28. Maughan, "Gossip Girl's Got Legs," 21.

29. "Gossip Girl," *The CW*, www.cwtv.com/thecw/gossip-girl (accessed July 17, 2007).

30. Nussbaum, "Psst, Serena is a Slut. Pass It On," 43.

31. Cecily Von Ziegesar, "From Cecily Von Ziegesar," *Gossip Girl: It Had to Be You: The Gossip Girl Prequel*, www.amazon.com/review/R2AWN4C13RV7 HU/ref=cm_cr_rdp_perm (accessed November 26, 2007).

32. Naomi Wolf, "Wild Things," *New York Times Book Review*, (March 12, 2006): 22.

33. Colleen Long, "What a Girl Wants: Company Churning Out Books, TV Pilots, Films with Teen-Girl Appeal," *Akron Beacon Journal*, www.ohio.com/ mld/beaconjournal/living/12092984.htm?template (accessed April 28, 2006).

34. Wolf, "Wild Things," 22.

35. Pattee, "Commodities in Literature, Literature as Commodity," 171.

36. Laura Sessions Stepp, *Unhooked: How Young Women Pursue Sex, Delay Love, and Lose at Both* (New York: Riverhead Books, 2007), 24.

37. Stepp, *Unhooked*, 62.

38. Pattee, "Commodities in Literature, Literature as Commodity," 168.

39. Wolf, "Wild Things," 22.

40. Patty Campbell, "The Sand in the Oyster: The *Lit* of Chick Lit," *Horn Book*, 82.4 (July/August 2006): 491.

41. Campbell, "The Sand in the Oyster: The *Lit* of Chick Lit," 491.

42. Campbell, "The Sand in the Oyster: The *Lit* of Chick Lit," 487.

43. Wolf, "Wild Things," 23.

44. John Barlow, "I Coulda Been a Pretender: How I Didn't End Up Like That Harvard Sophomore Accused of Plagiarizing Her Novel," *Slate*, www.slate.com/id/2140620 (accessed April 27, 2006).

45. Pattee, "Commodities in Literature, Literature as Commodity," 168.

46. Leslie Bennetts, *The Feminine Mistake* (New York: Hyperion, 2007), 38.

47. Kolhatkar, "Viswanathan-athon."

48. Sally Beatty, "Books: You're Reading . . . What?" *Wall Street Journal*, (June 24, 2005): W1.

Appendix A: Alphabetical List of Series

This section includes a list of the series studied in this book. Series authors are included. Author pseudonyms are indicated with the abbreviation pseud. after the name.

Series Name	Publisher	Author	Dates
The A-List	Little, Brown	Zoey Dean (pseud.)	2003–
Aunt Jane's Nieces	Reilly & Britton	Edith Van Dyne (pseud.)	1906–1918
The Automobile Girls	Altemus	Laura Dent Crane	1910–1913
The Baby-Sitters Club	Scholastic	Ann M. Martin	1986–2000
Balefire	Penguin	Cate Tiernan (pseud.)	2005–2006
Betty Gordon	Cupples & Leon	Alice B. Emerson (pseud.)	1920–1932
Betty Wales	Penn	Margaret Warde (pseud.)	1904–1917
Beverly Gray	A. L. Burt	Clair Blank	1934–1955
Billie Bradley	Sully	Janet D. Wheeler (pseud.)	1920–1932
Camp Fire Girls	Winston	Margaret Vandercook	1913–1921
Chain Letter	Simon & Schuster	Christopher Pike (pseud.)	1986–1992
Cherry Ames	Grosset & Dunlap	Helen Wells, Julie Tatham	1943–1968
The Clique	Little, Brown	Lisi Harrison	2004–
Connie Blair	Grosset & Dunlap	Betsy Allen (pseud.)	1948–1958
The Dana Girls	Grosset & Dunlap	Carolyn Keene (pseud.)	1934–1979
Dinny Gordon	Macrae Smith	Anne Emery	1959–1965
Dorothy Dale	Cupples & Leon	Margaret Penrose (pseud.)	1908–1924
Elizabeth	Bantam	Francine Pascal (creator)	2001
Elsie Dinsmore	Dodd, Mead	Martha Finley (pseud.)	1867–1905

Series Name	Publisher	Author	Dates
Fear Street	Simon & Schuster	R. L. Stine	1989–1999
Fearless	Simon & Schuster	Francine Pascal	1999–2004
Fearless FBI	Simon & Schuster	Francine Pascal	2005–2006
First Love	Silhouette	Various	1981–1987
Ginny Gordon	Whitman	Julie Campbell	1948–1956
The Girls of Central High	Grosset & Dunlap	Gertrude W. Morrison (pseud.)	1914–1921
Gossip Girl	Little, Brown	Cecily Von Ziegesar (creator)	2002–
Grace Harlowe: The College Girls	Altemus	Jessie Graham Flower (pseud.)	1910–1911
Grace Harlowe: The High School Girls	Altemus	Jessie Graham Flower (pseud.)	1914–1917
Grace Harlowe Overseas Series	Altemus	Jessie Graham Flower (pseud.)	1920
Grace Harlowe's Overland Rider Series	Altemus	Jessie Graham Flower (pseud.)	1921–1924
Helen Grant	Lothrop, Lee & Shepard	Amanda M. Douglas	1903–1911
The It Girl	Little, Brown	Cecily Von Ziegesar (creator)	2005–
Jane Allen	Cupples & Leon	Edith Bancroft	1917–1922
Jessica Darling	Random House	Megan McCafferty	2001–
Judy Bolton	Grosset & Dunlap	Margaret Sutton	1932–1967
Kay Tracey	Cupples & Leon	Frances K. Judd (pseud.)	1934–1942
Linda Craig	Doubleday	Ann Sheldon	1962–1964
Love Stories	Bantam	Various	1995–2001
Marcy Rhodes	Lippincott	Rosamund Du Jardin	1950–1957
Marjorie Dean	A. L. Burt	Pauline Lester (pseud.)	1917–1930
The Motor Girls	Cupples & Leon	Margaret Penrose (pseud.)	1910–1917
Nancy Drew	Grosset & Dunlap	Carolyn Keene (pseud.)	1930–2003
Nancy Drew Files	Simon & Schuster	Carolyn Keene (pseud.)	1986–1997
Nancy Drew on Campus	Simon & Schuster	Carolyn Keene (pseud.)	1995–1998
The Outdoor Girls	Grosset & Dunlap	Laura Lee Hope (pseud.)	1913–1933
Pam and Penny Howard	Lippincott	Rosamund Du Jardin	1951–1959
Pat Marlowe	Westminster	Anne Emery	1956–1958
Penny Parker	Cupples & Leon	Mildred A. Wirt	1939–1947
Parrish Family	Grosset & Dunlap	Janet Lambert	1941–1969
The Princess Diaries	HarperCollins	Meg Cabot	2000–
Private	Simon & Schuster	Kate Brian (pseud.)	2006–
The Red Cross Girls	Winston	Margaret Vandercook	1916–1920

Series Name	Publisher	Author	Dates
River Heights	Simon & Schuster	Carolyn Keene (pseud.)	1989–1992
Ruth Fielding	Cupples & Leon	Alice B. Emerson (pseud.)	1913–1934
Samurai Girl	Simon & Schuster	Carrie Asai	2003–2004
Sisterhood of the Traveling Pants	Delacorte	Ann Brashares	2001–
Sue Barton	Little, Brown	Helen Dore Boylston	1936–1952
SVH Senior Year	Bantam	Francine Pascal (creator)	1999–2003
Sweep	Penguin	Cate Tiernan (pseud.)	2001–2003
Sweet Dreams	Bantam	Various	1981–1995
Sweet Valley High	Bantam	Kate William (pseud.)	1983–1998
Sweet Valley University	Bantam	Laurie John (pseud.)	1993–2000
Three Vassar Girls	Estes & Lauriat	Elizabeth W. Champney	1882–1892
Tobey and Midge Heydon	Lippincott	Rosamud Du Jardin	1949–1961
Trixie Belden	Whitman	Julie Campbell	1948–1986
T*Witches	Scholastic	Randi Reisfeld, H. B. Gilmour	2001–2004
Vicki Barr	Grosset & Dunlap	Helen Wells, Julie Tatham	1947–1964
Wildfire	Scholastic	Various	1979–1986

Appendix B:
Important Books about Girls' Series Fiction

Axe, John. *All about Collecting Girls' Series Books*. Grantsville, MD: Hobby House, 2002.

——. *The Secret of Collecting Girls' Series Books*. Grantsville, MD: Hobby House, 2000.

Billman, Carol. *The Secret of the Stratemeyer Syndicate*. New York: Ungar, 1986.

Christian-Smith, Linda. *Becoming a Woman through Romance*. New York: Routledge, 1990.

Dyer, Carolyn Stewart, and Nancy Tillman Romalov, eds. *Rediscovering Nancy Drew*. Iowa City: University of Iowa Press, 1995.

Inness, Sherrie A., ed. *Nancy Drew and Company: Culture, Gender, and Girls' Series*. Bowling Green, OH: Bowling Green State University Popular Press, 1997.

Johnson, Deidre. *Edward Stratemeyer and the Stratemeyer Syndicate*. New York: Twayne, 1993.

Kismaric, Carole, and Marvin Heiferman. *The Mysterious Case of Nancy Drew and the Hardy Boys*. New York: Fireside, 1998.

Makowski, Silk. *Serious about Series: Evaluations and Annotations of Teen Fiction in Paperback Series*. Lanham, MD: Scarecrow, 1998.

Mason, Bobbie Ann. *The Girl Sleuth*. 2nd ed. Athens: University of Georgia Press, 1995.

Rehak, Melanie. *Girl Sleuth: Nancy Drew and the Women Who Created Her*. Orlando, FL: Harcourt, 2005.

Society of Phantom Friends. *The Girls' Series Companion*. Rheem Valley, CA: SynSine, 1997.

Index

Pam and Penny Howard series, 87, 120–21

paperback originals, 114–15

parental reactions, 117

Parrish Family series, 66, 67–72, 85–88, 102–3

Parry, Sally E., 73, 75

Pascal, Francine: Alloy Inc. and, 146; girl power and, 138–39; 17st Street Productions, 130; success of, 114, 122, 133; Sweet Valley creator, 120–21. *See also* Sweet Valley High series

Pat Marlowe series, 87, 104

Pattee, Amy, 143, 144, 145

Penny Nichols series, 61

Penny Parker series, 61–62, 72

Penrose, Margaret, 35

Phelps, Elizabeth Stuart, 2

Pike, Christopher, 129, 133

plagiarism scandals, 147

The Princess Diaries series, 146

Private series, 142–43

Quinnebasset series, 2

racism, 5–9, 85, 95

realism, 91, 97, 101, 121

Rehak, Melanie, xvi, 44, 45, 46, 51, 53, 54, 55, 61, 125

River Heights series, 126

Rollin, Lucy, 37, 66, 92

Romalov, Nancy Tillman, 33, 37, 40

romance series: Campfire Girls, 39; careers and, 24, 78–79, 103–4, 105; Cherry Ames, 75; heterosexual relationships and, 25; Nancy Drew and, 126; of 1940s, 67–72; of 1950s, 85–92, 98; of 1960s, 102–5; of 1980s, 115–24, 126; paperback originals, 115; soap operas and, 120–24, 130–33

romanticism, 1

Ross, Catherine Sheldrick, xii–xiii

Ruth Fielding series, 29, 34, 40–44

Samson, Emma Speed, 25

Scholastic Book Services, 116, 117

schoolgirls, 13–14. *See also* all-around girls; college girls; Gibson girls; high school athletes

Scott, Kieran, 142

sentimentalism, 1

series: advertising campaigns, 107–8, 118–20; alphabetical list, 151–53; appeal of, xi–xii, 12, 92, 147; criticisms of, xiii; defined, xii; research on, xv–xvi, 155; trends, xiii–xv

17th Street Productions, 129–30, 140–41

sexuality: avoidance of, 109–11; in Betty Wales series, 22; heterosexual relationships, 25; incestuous implications, 4, 57; in 1950s, 91–92; in soap operas, 122, 123 24

Silhouette, 115, 118–19, 122

Simon & Schuster, 112, 124–25

Singleton, Ellen, 25, 28, 39

Sisterhood of the Traveling Pants series, 140

slaves, 5

sleuths: Betty Gordon, 45–46; Beverly Gray, 50, 60–61, 67, 72, 94; Cherry Ames, 73–76, 79, 93, 106–7, 137; The Dana Girls, 55, 56–57, 94, 109; Ginny Gordon, 80–81; Judy Bolton, 49–50, 58–60,

About the Author

Carolyn Carpan is director of Public Services in the Burke Library at Hamilton College in Clinton, New York. She received graduate degrees in library and information studies from Dalhousie University in Nova Scotia and women's studies from the Memorial University of Newfoundland. Her previous books include *Rocked by Romance: A Guide to Teen Romance Fiction* (2004) and *Jane Yolen* (2005).